CAT + NAT'S

Mom
Truths

CAT & NAT'S

Mom Truths

EMBARRASSING STORIES and
BRUTALLY HONEST ADVICE
on the EXTREMELY REAL
STRUGGLE of MOTHERHOOD

CATHERINE BELKNAP
NATALIE TELFER

HARMONY
BOOKS · NEW YORK

Library of Congress Cataloging-in-Publication Data

Names: Belknap, Catherine, author. | Telfer, Natalie, author.
Title: Cat & Nat's mom truths: embarrassing stories and brutally honest
advice on the extremely real struggle of motherhood /
Catherine Belknap & Natalie Telfer.
Other titles: Cat and Nat's mom truths | Cat & Nat's mom truths
Description: New York: Harmony Books, [2019]
Identifiers: LCCN 2018036757 | ISBN 9780525574910 (pbk.)
Subjects: LCSH: Motherhood. | Motherhood—Humor.
Classification: LCC HQ759 .B4445 2019 | DDC 306.874/3—dc23
LC record available at https://lccn.loc.gov/2018036757

ISBN 978-0-525-57491-0
Ebook ISBN 978-0-525-57492-7

Printed in the United States of America

Book design by Nancy Singer
Flame emojis by Vecteezy.com, Instagram profile photograph by Marianne Rothbauer,
and Instagram post photograph by Lee Hon Bong
Cat and Nat illustrations by Brook Coppola
Cover design by Matt Chase
Cover photographs: (doll) Matt Chase; (wine) sarasang/E+/Getty Images

10 9 8 7 6 5 4 3 2 1

First US Edition

For our seven (!) children . . .
and for moms everywhere

Contents

CONTENTS

ONE

Welcome to the Shitshow

Hello, Moms! Or Moms-to-Be! Or some random dad who picked up this book by mistake. (Put the book down, Dad. This isn't for you. Unless you're trying to figure out what's going on with your lady so that you can better serve her, in which case: Read on, hero.)

Ladies, if you know who we are—if you've seen our famous YouTube videos, if you follow us on Instagram or Facebook, if you've been to one of our live FUN Shows—then welcome! We're so glad you're here with us. We are psyched to share our stories and our, um, wisdom with you.

If you have no clue who we are, well . . . where the heck to start?

We're Cat and Nat! On the surface, it can be a little hard to tell us apart: two moms, two blondes, two extroverts (the polite term for "motormouths"). Our names rhyme, just to make things even more confusing. So let's try to clear things up right off the bat:

A CAT & NAT CHEAT SHEET
Who the heck is who?

NAT	CAT
Long nails	Short nails
Heels	Flip-flops
Long flowing hair	Ponytail almost always
Constantly lost and confused	Always walks about a step ahead of Nat because Nat never knows where the hell she's going
Wine	Tequila
Can drink Cat (and most men) under the table	Gets drunk off one shot
Hates to drive, and almost never drives on the highway	Drives all the time because, well, someone has to
Great chef and picks all the best restaurants	Orders McDonald's cheeseburgers without the meat
Phone is somehow always at 2% battery	Phone is always fully charged for maximum Instagram readiness
Talks a lot	Talks even more

We hung out a fair bit in high school, but we weren't BFFs. A decade later, we became the first of our group of friends to have kids, and we both found it so much to handle. We felt like failures a lot of the time. We stressed and we beat ourselves up. But we found comfort and confidence in one another.

Today, we are best friends who have seven (!) young kids between us. Nat has four and Cat has three—although to be honest, it's usually just the nine of us together as a roaming pack of noise, mischief, and chaos. We live near each other in Toronto. We are married to guys named Mark and Marc. Yes, really. They hang out with each other, too, and we assume they spend most of their time talking about how lucky they are and how well they married. ;-)

We are not helicopter parents or Tiger Moms or whatever kind of overbearing mother is trendy right now. We are not parenting "experts" (whatever that means). We haven't studied at some fancy school. But we have been in the Mom trenches for a decade, and here's what we *do* know:

- We know what it's like to hear your baby start wailing in the middle of the night, four minutes after you fed and changed her.
- We know how it feels to ask yourself the question "Is 4:30 p.m. too early to send the kids to bed?"
- We know the comedy of not being able to go to the bathroom without your children following along. You just want forty-five seconds to pee in peace and suddenly it's a family meeting in there!
- We know about husbands who want sex, and children who want a seventeenth bedtime story, and the other tightly wound moms out there who want to make you feel inferior because you didn't stay

up until 2:00 a.m. baking organic, gluten-free, sugar-free, artisanal scones for the school bake sale.

In other words, we know the reality of motherhood. That's why we've written a book that's easy to pick up, easy to read—and easy to put down when you hear the sound of one thousand Rice Krispies hitting the floor in the kitchen. Come back to us whenever you can find a free minute or two. We'll be here waiting.

We also know that being a mom can change who you are, and not always for the better. Like a lot of mothers, we went through a phase where we tried to mimic the seemingly perfect moms of the world. We became overanxious, overly controlling overanalyzers. Somehow, we managed to be incredibly self-conscious *and* to judge other moms at the same time! We had to let go of that nonsense, and we are here to help you do the same thing.

Lots of days, we felt like we were barely hanging on. Then we found each other—and, just as important, we found a new attitude. We started laughing at the absurdity of it all. We bonded over the hardships and the hilarity of motherhood. After a while, we kept coming back to the idea of helping other moms deal with the challenges and the stress and the isolation that motherhood can bring. That's why we started making our little videos. That's probably how you know us, those four-minute videos of us sitting in a car and talking—sometimes ranting . . . okay, *usually* ranting—about motherhood and its challenges and frustrations and its awesome moments and whatever else comes into our heads. Sometimes we dance in the car. Often there are props. It can get a little crazy. And yes, from time to time, people who are walking by on the sidewalk stop and stare and snap a few photos of the two nutcases bopping around in a parked SUV.

It all grew from there. Now we are part of a community of women—moms who celebrate who they are, how they raise their kids, and how they treat themselves. We want to share that experience with you. We want you to join us. So be sure to hit us up on Facebook or Instagram and let us know what you think of the book. We are easy to find.

Our goal is to make you laugh when you're feeling low, inspire you when you're feeling overwhelmed, and reassure you when you're feeling defeated. We are not going to lecture you or make you feel bad about yourself or any of your decisions. (That's what the Internet is for!) We want to support you. We want to build people up. We want to make motherhood a sisterhood!

As we said earlier, we've got seven kids between us. And here's the ridiculous thing: We still don't have all the answers. Not even close! We're figuring it out in real time. We're flailing and failing a lot of the time. So if you're looking for some flawless, superbrainy parenting advice, you are going to want to step slowly away from this book! But we've got a lot of experiences to share, stories to tell, and maybe a few thousand mistakes to laugh about.

We are finally in a place where we can write the book that we desperately wanted to read when *we* first became mothers. An honest and candid book for mothers who don't necessarily have a Cat or a Nat to call up—but want to know they're not alone. Something to help moms through the hard times. A book that says: The struggle is real. It's huge and it's overwhelming and it's disorienting. But you can do this. You can *definitely* do this.

We can do it together.

Okay, there's one last thing we want to tell you before we get started. In this book, we are going to talk a bit about husbands because we happen to be married to guys (and not to each other, as some people assume—though we *would* make a hot, kick-ass couple). But when we mention our hubs, you can just sub in whatever applies to you: boyfriend, wife, life partner, girlfriend, significant other, full-size Ryan Reynolds cardboard cutout, whatever. We are down with however you live and whomever you love.

And we bow down to the single moms. Both Nat and I come from families where our parents split up and got divorced. And both of our mothers were extremely independent and self-reliant. That's where we both learned to respect the strength of an independent woman. It's awe-inspiring what women can accomplish without anyone's help. If you're on this journey without a partner, you're amazing.

All right, here we go! We don't have motherhood all figured out. But we are ready to get honest and real with you about the ridiculous, amazing, fulfilling, frustrating, life-altering, soul-stirring, headache-inducing gong show of being a mom—and all it brings in terms of pressures and pain and joy and frustration, fun and heartache and laundry. Don't get us started on the damn laundry!

And remember: It's gonna be okay. ***You're gonna be okay!***

Cat & Nat
Toronto, 2019

TWO

Bad News, Ladies: The End of the Delivery Is Just the Beginning

CAT

The morning after I gave birth to our first child, I woke up with fifty stitches in my vagina and a question in my head: "Catherine, what the hell have you gotten yourself into?"

Barely a day earlier, we'd been at a rehearsal dinner for a friend's wedding. It was late. I was grumpy because everyone else was wasted and laughing and I couldn't drink. That's when labor hit. It hit hard— and so did a huge wave of fear and panic. The idyllic "I'm going to have a baby!" suddenly became the terrifying "I'm going to have to deliver a baby through my body!" I'll never forget what happened next. I leaned over to my husband, squeezed his hand, and whispered in his ear: "I'm not sure I want to do this anymore."

A little late to back out now, Cat.

And besides, it was definitely time to get on with it. I was two weeks past my due date. For a couple months, I'd spent most of my time feeling either gigantic or homicidal. Sometimes both. *Usually* both.

I know some people probably think Canada is cold all the time. But Toronto in summertime is like living inside a dryer filled with wet towels. It's hot. It's moist. It's supernoisy. You're sweating all the time. Which makes carrying around another entire person inside of you such a huge pleasure, she says sarcastically. I knew we were in uncharted territory when I discovered one morning that I could no longer see my vaheen. It was lost somewhere between my stomach and my thighs. That seventy pounds of extra weight was not my friend.

Marc and I lived in a tiny little house on a dead-end street. We were one of those annoying couples that had a dog we treated like a child. We'd dress him up on Halloween and even give him gifts on

Christmas morning. Yep, we were pretty insufferable. I'm sure more than a few strangers rolled their eyes at us, but I didn't care. I was honing my maternal instincts!

In those final couple months, when I basically weighed a metric tonne and couldn't fit into any clothes and most automobiles, it is possible that I maybe got a little grumpy from time to time. I remember one night my husband made the mistake of asking why I was always so tired. We were sitting at our little kitchen table, and my first instinct was to jab a fork into his arm. He didn't really mean anything by it, I'm sure. He probably said it without thinking. (Men are great at that.) But do you think I was going to let him off the hook? Not a frickin' chance! I gave it to him with both barrels. "Oh, I'm sorry if I'm a little tired since I spent all day growing *another human person* inside of me. Growing their organs and their fingers and every other part of them. *I grew part of a brain today!* What did *you* do?"

Most times when there is shouting in a marriage, it ends in a draw or in an uneasy truce—but I think it's safe to say I won that one. Decisively. Feel free to steal the "growing a human person" card and use it yourself. You can't lose.

For the whole time I was pregnant, and even a bit before, I had this very clear image in my head: Life with a baby was going to be so perfect. My husband and I would lie in bed together with the baby between us and we'd hold hands. We'd go to pumpkin patches and we'd be so cute and everyone would think to themselves, "Now there are a couple of parents who've got it all together, posing on a haystack in their flannel with their apple cider donuts, looking all adorable."

Fast-forward to my tenth hour of labor. I'm in agony. Meanwhile, my husband and my doctor are down at the end of the bed, making small talk about hockey. I wanted to murder them both. I'm not even sure that I'm joking. If only they'd been just a little bit closer, I might have reached out and clocked them with a bedpan. I know that sounds kind of harsh, but believe me: It's hard to be your calm, regular self when a human being is trying to push her way into the world through your vagina. You're bound to be a little on edge.

Eventually, the epidural worked its magic. I managed a couple hours of enthusiastic pushing/profanity. I even remember the August sun coming out and shining into the hospital room just before our little girl was born. The whole thing turned out kind of great, to be honest. I remember thinking to myself: "I did it! Mission accomplished! Hooray for me!" I even managed to crack a joke. When the doctor went to work on repairing my vagina, he said that he was going to "sew [me] back up like Mother Nature intended." Without missing a beat, I said, "Can you make it a little tighter than she intended?"

I was pumped. I had gotten through it. My pregnancy was over at last!

Turns out the end of the delivery was just the beginning.

Goodbye, excitement; hello, exhaustion. So long, anticipation; hello, anxiety. I wasn't ready for any of it. From the second that Olivia was born, I felt an overwhelming urge to go home. I wanted to set a land speed record for getting out of a hospital. But first, I had to pass a test.

I had to pass the fart test.

They gave me the whole explanation, but I wasn't really listening, due to the exhaustion and the precious new human life that was suddenly taking up all my brain space. Basically, it was about making sure everything was working down there after the epidural and the trauma of the delivery. Bottom line: I had to fart before they would agree to discharge me. Now, just to be clear, it's not like they post a nurse at your bedside and give her a Geiger counter for fart monitoring. They take your word for it.

This is an important piece of information, because I was *obsessed* with getting out of there. So I decided to exploit the loophole in the system. Translation: I lied. I told them I had farted. But I hadn't farted. People lie about farting all the time, but this may have marked the first time in human history that anyone ever lied to take credit for a fart.

They believed me. My fake fart set me free. As my husband started packing up all our stuff, I put my feet on the floor and pushed my way out of bed so I could get changed, practically able to feel the sweet air of freedom on my cheeks. And then I went down like a ton of bricks. Turns out the epidural hadn't totally worn off—or maybe it was the painkillers they were giving me on account of my poor, damaged vagina. Either way, my legs were basically a couple of gummy worms.

Looking back, I think of this as the first of roughly 28,000 mistakes I've made as a mother. I can't even remember why I was so eager to leave. I should have just stayed in bed and let those farts rip.

After fifteen minutes or so, I got the feeling back in my legs. I could stand on my own. As I left the hospital, less than forty-eight hours after giving birth, they gave me an ice pack and a baby. Our beautiful baby. Our beautiful, crying Olivia. And that was it. Were they really just going to let me go off into the world and be a mother? Couldn't they tell I had absolutely no idea what I was doing? I had faked a fart test!

The days that followed were a blur. I mean that literally. I was so tired that I had trouble seeing things in focus. It wasn't how I thought it was going to be. I can't actually remember if Marc and I ever lay in bed with the baby between us, holding hands and being all cute. I can tell you we definitely never made it to a pumpkin patch.

For the six weeks after our daughter was born, I was basically a hermit. I became a self-imposed shut-in. I was afraid to leave the house with the baby. Too many scary and dangerous things out there in the world!

Or maybe I stayed in because I didn't want the world to catch on to the fact that, when it came to being a mom, I just didn't have a clue. What if my baby cried? What if *I* cried? Everyone else seemed to always have it together, and I was hanging on by a thread.

I'd walk circles around our living room, holding our daughter. Twenty minutes. Forty minutes. Two hours. The baby wouldn't stop crying. I'd try swaddling her using the zillion different techniques and methods that people swear by on the Internet. None of them worked—she wouldn't stop crying. I'd put the baby down and walk out of the room for a breather, only to rush back in because I was scared by how loudly she was crying. I'd beg my husband to come home from work and help out. The baby wouldn't stop crying. Feed the baby. Hold the baby. Put the baby down. Pick the baby up. It didn't matter. *The baby wouldn't stop crying.* I felt like a fuckup.

In those early moments, I came to understand why some women simply fall apart at the seams. The first six weeks can be hell—especially if you're like me and you get into your own head. It goes like this: "This is *my* responsibility. She is my responsibility and I'm screwing it up. You're screwing it up, Cat." You feel it every time your baby cries. You feel it every time you can't figure out what's wrong with her. You feel it every time your baby is wailing in public and people are looking at you, like, "Hey, can you stop being a terrible mother for just a minute and make your baby be quiet?" You feel the heat of all those eyes staring at you and judging you. You actually start to sweat. And you don't know what to do to make the baby stop crying, because you've tried everything. You wonder why you don't have any maternal instincts. You feel like a failure. I felt like a failure.

At my lowest point, I can remember feeling as though I was stuck in a snow globe. Just when everything finally started to feel settled, my whole world would get shaken up again. And I was powerless to stop it because I was stuck in the game of "perfect," just like every other mom. My only outlet was taking to Facebook to ask perfectly normal, concerned parent questions like, "Does anyone have any suggestions for good sleep training materials?" Which really meant, "I'm not getting any sleep. I'm going out of my mind. Someone send help." And then I thumbed through the comments as I sat in an old T-shirt covered in vomit (not mine) and food stains (mostly mine, to be honest). Scroll, scroll, scroll. And then I saw a message notification.

It was a message from my old friend Natalie, whom I'd barely seen since high school. She'd had a baby of her own eight months earlier. Her message was very direct: "Get over here. *Now!*" Naturally, I said no. Going to someone's house meant . . . gasp . . . going outside! And outside is where the sun is, and the bugs, and strangers and trucks and germs and noises and surprises. Nat wouldn't take no for an answer. Thank God she wouldn't.

It took me fifteen minutes just to get the stroller into the car. I'd never broken it down before because I'd never gone anywhere with the baby. I cursed the stroller. I cursed my own lack of mothering skills. Mostly I cursed Nat for making me do this. But a few minutes later, I was standing on Natalie's front porch. She opened the door. She looked at me, and she just knew. "Come on in," she said. "You look like shit."

It was the first time I'd laughed in weeks.

Natalie and I talked for hours that day. She answered all my questions. To be honest, she probably answered most of them at least twice. I kept repeating myself thanks to my clouded mom brain.

Nat had a handle on the parenting thing. It had taken her a while, but she'd figured it out. That's how it seemed to me, at least. I know this much for certain: She had definitely brushed her hair at some point in the previous seventy-two hours, which is more than I could say for myself.

Nat and I started walking together with our babies once or twice a week. Then pretty much every day. For hours at a time. I felt like I could talk to her about anything. About *everything*. For the first time since I gave birth, I felt that I could be honest with someone. Nothing was off-limits. If you happened to pass by us on one of our epic walks, you probably heard us complaining about swollen boobs or debating the best balm for cracked nipples. You know, supersexy talk. We must have sounded crazy. We definitely *looked* crazy— messy hair, mismatched socks. But those walks and those conversations saved me.

Once I found Natalie, my loneliness lifted. The baby's crying became more bearable. Sometimes I even managed to laugh through the stress of it all. I was no longer sinking. Nat was my life raft.

It wasn't that my husband didn't try to be supportive. He just didn't get it. He *couldn't* get it. He couldn't understand what I was going through on an emotional level—a biological level. He couldn't understand why I had *zero* interest in sex, or even in being touched. I remember saying to Nat as we embarked on an epic walk in the middle of a snowstorm: "How come no one warned us about this? How come no one warned us about the isolation and the feeling that we'll just never figure things out?"

Today, almost a decade later, we look back on that first afternoon at Natalie's house as the beginning of the playdate that never ended. We've learned so much from one another. But mostly, we've learned so much *together*.

THREE

Macaulay Culkin Ruined My Life

Nat

When things are utterly crazy around our house—when the kids are all losing their shit at the exact same time and my head feels like it is literally going to explode—I think back on our decision to have four children, and I blame one person and one person only.

I blame Macaulay Culkin.

It's all his fault. As a little girl, I saw the movie *Home Alone,* and it changed my life. No, I didn't rush home and booby-trap my house in case Joe Pesci decided to break in. I left the movie focused on something very different: the little boy's family. His huge family.

I knew it the moment I saw it: That's what I want. I want the large family. I want the chaos and the bickering and the fighting for the bathroom. I want people talking over each other and never finding a moment's peace. I want a family so big that I could leave one of my kids behind and not even notice until I'm halfway across the Atlantic. I want to be part of a frantic, combative bunch that nevertheless bonds together and fights like hell for one another when the going gets tough. One big team to take on the world.

Later, when I was a teenager, this feeling was reinforced when a new family moved in down the street—a husband and wife in their early thirties with four kids. Today, I remember very little about the wife. I remember *a lot* about the husband. He was a classic Hot Dad—great body, tall and fit, liked to jog. It's possible that I may have lingered by the front window in the mornings in the hope of seeing him run past. It's also possible that I spent a year or two silently hoping the wife would get some horrible disease. Nothing painful, of course—but definitely 100 percent fatal. Believe me, I was ready to console the widower.

But seriously, they were a great family. They had the nice house. They had well-behaved children. He had awesome abs. I wanted all those things. I already knew I wanted a big family. Now I knew how many kids I wanted: four. Exactly four. Just like Mr. and Mrs. Hot Dad.

I don't want you to get the wrong idea: I wasn't *obsessed* with having kids. I didn't show up for a date with a clipboard and a questionnaire about "preferred number of children." But at the same time, that image of the "perfect family" never really faded from my mind.

When I got married at twenty-seven (see, I didn't rush it!), I wanted to have a baby right away. Like, to the point that I was thinking: "Let's cut this wedding reception short and adjourn to the honeymoon suite." No point in wasting time, right? Only one problem: My husband wasn't as psyched. Mark wanted to spend some time together as a married couple—just the two of us. At least a few years before starting a family. Being a good and understanding partner, I said, Okay, fine, I'll wait a few years. And then I basically nagged him about having a baby so much and so often that he finally gave in. I think he may have actually thrown up his hands in frustration. I can be a real pain in the ass.

Among my group of friends, I was the first to get married—the first to get pregnant, too. It's kind of awesome to be the First because you get fawned over and you get the big, fancy shower and you get everyone asking you all kinds of questions because you're the "expert" now. You're first and no one can catch up.

I liked it. I liked the attention. I liked being the pioneer of the group. I wasn't worried in the slightest about the delivery. That sounds weird, but it's true. I guess it's because my mom had told me that her labor was a piece of cake. It never occurred to me that it might not be the same for me.

After my water broke, I walked into the delivery room and

thought, "Wow." The place was like a luxury hotel. *Huge*. A big Jacuzzi tub over in the corner. Speakers on the wall so a future mom could blast her favorite playlist. I felt like a high roller in Las Vegas getting comped in a penthouse suite. Everyone doted on me. It felt like a spa getaway.

From the moment I arrived, I made it clear to the nurses: I had no interest in being a hero. I didn't want a war story of pain and perseverance. As much as I trusted my mom, I had seen enough hospital shows on TV to know that I wanted the epidural. I wanted two epidurals. *Give me all the epidurals!* I said the word so often that I'm pretty sure my nurse thought to herself: "This woman thinks my name is Epidural." I totally admire any woman who chooses natural childbirth. If you are one, I'm in awe of you. I am blown away by your courage. But I'm even more blown away by the scientists who figured out how a needle jabbed into my spine can make the pain go away. Those people are the real heroes. I am definitely Team Epidural.

Every mother has a labor story. My belief is that no one *really* wants to hear it. It's kind of like a guy talking about his fantasy baseball roster to his friends—they'll listen, but they don't really care. So I'll spare you the details and just say: I nailed it. My baby was cute and healthy and I felt good. We named her Taylor. After an hour or so, we invited our friends and family into the room. I'm not talking about a few people—I'm talking about a busload. We welcomed them in, and our delivery room became a party suite. Hooray for the First! Hugs were exchanged. Champagne bottles were popped. We even ordered takeout! I remember saying to a friend, "That was a breeze. I'm ready to have another."

Twelve hours later, the party was over. They wheeled me out of

the superposh delivery suite and into a cramped hospital room—
a room that had peeling paint and a weird smell and a whole other
person. Someone I didn't know. Someone who was making loud
noises, as though she was in pain. So much for the spa/VIP suite/
party bus experience.

It was the middle of the night, but I was wide awake and super-
stressed, in part because of the moaning from across the room but
also because my baby wouldn't eat. She just didn't seem interested.

I had this one nurse who must have skipped the day in school
when they taught bedside manner. She'd come into the room with
my baby, and without saying a word she'd plop Taylor down on my
chest. Then she'd grab my boob and try to aim the nipple at my
baby's mouth. I don't want to sound like a prude or anything, but this
made me really uncomfortable. No woman had ever touched one of
my boobs before! I mean, on a logical level I totally get that women's
breasts are just part of a typical day at work for a nurse in the mater-
nity ward. But for some reason it felt like an invasion. I *so* wanted to
get out of there. I asked to be discharged. Nurse Boob Grabber was
predictably curt in her reply: "You can't go home because your baby
is losing weight."

That's when I really started freaking out. I was the First of my
friends to be freaking out. I'm not going to lie to you: I went a little
bit diva. I started demanding a private room. How can I possibly
feed my baby with all those *weird lady noises* coming from behind the
curtain? Not a good look, Nat.

Most of the nurses just nodded and said supportive things. They'd
probably been through this a billion times before—but I was still
overwhelmed by everything they were making me do. I had to wake

up every two hours to pump breast milk. They said they were also going to give my baby a bottle of formula—which of course made me lose my mind because my entire life we've been told, *breast milk good, formula bad*. I was stressed and tired and anxious and angry, but more than anything else, I felt inadequate—like I'd let down my baby on her first day in the world. I remember saying out loud to myself in the middle of the night, as I pumped breast milk in the dark and a lady I'd never seen moaned ten feet away from me: "Nat, this is hell."

I thought it would get better when we finally got home. It didn't. Our baby cried all night long. *I* cried all night long. I hardly ever slept. I felt so lonely. My husband was right there, but I still felt lonely. My friends called and texted and dropped by, but I still felt lonely, even when I was with a group of people.

My friends didn't know what I was going through. They didn't know what to ask. They didn't understand why I'd break down and cry in front of them. They must have thought I was a crazy person. Suddenly, it didn't seem so great to be the First.

During the day, my baby would fall asleep only when she was lying on me. Not ideal for a lot of reasons. It's hard to get the laundry done when you're flat on your back. During the night, Taylor wouldn't fall asleep at all. It would be three o'clock in the morning, or four o'clock, or one o'clock—the hours blended together into the fog of half sleep. I would hold my baby and stand by the window in our living room. I would look out at the apartment building off in the distance. And I would think to myself, "Is anybody out there? Is anyone awake? Is anybody out there going through what I'm going through? Because I feel like I'm the only person in the world who's feeling what I'm feeling."

Morning came (eventually). I would wake up exhausted. I was hardly eating. My diet pretty much consisted in its entirety of jujubes and Toblerone chocolate. I don't think I'm going to get approached to write a cookbook anytime soon.

Here's a feeling I'll never forget: I would spend most of the day waiting for my husband to get home. I would stare at the clock and try to use my mind to speed up the passage of time. If you haven't had your baby yet, this probably doesn't make sense to you. It seemed perfectly reasonable to me.

I would have given anything for that man of mine to walk in the door an hour ahead of schedule. But here's the thing: When he *finally* did get home . . . I still wanted to be in control of the baby. I just couldn't shut off my mothering impulses.

Naturally, this was all pretty confusing for Mark. *Hey, crazy lady, you begged me to come home and help with the baby—and now you're not letting me help with the baby.* I guess in the end I just wanted someone there to be unhappy with me. What a bonding experience—come be miserable with me, honey!

My mom got pretty worried. She could see that I was struggling. She tried to help, but I wouldn't let her. She tried to give me advice, but I ignored it. (Did I mention that I can be a pain in the ass?) Finally, my mom basically forced me to go and see a doctor. He gave me a prescription. Something to help me cope. I don't feel proud admitting this, but I don't feel ashamed, either. It's what I needed at the time. And it made a big difference. I had more patience. More energy. I was able to get myself and my baby into a routine—and that made an even bigger difference. We'd go on a morning walk. We'd hang out at the park with all the nannies. My little girl was way too young to play, but I liked going there because the nannies were always so calm and they were never in distress. They became my role models! Nothing ever fazed them.

By the time Cat had her baby, I finally felt like I'd managed to get things under control. I was sleeping for hours at a time at night. I didn't feel like a pro, exactly—but I no longer felt like a rookie. I wasn't an Olympian, but I wasn't drowning anymore, either.

I remember seeing Cat's post. At the time we were Facebook friends, which means we weren't really friends at all. We were acquaintances. But I knew instantly what she was feeling. And I knew that most of her close friends wouldn't be able to understand or help. It was time for the First to share her wisdom!

Cat likes to say I saved her, that I was the lifeline she needed, but Cat was good for me, too. She reassured me when I was feeling a little defeated. And she made me laugh when I was bummed—which was so great, because it felt as though I hadn't laughed in years. We went from being Facebook friends, to real friends, to best friends.

And because of that friendship and support, I had the confidence and energy to build the large family that I'd always wanted. Four kids, just like the Hot Dad household. It's not quite as big as the *Home Alone* family, but there are times when it seems every bit as loud, every bit as frustrating, every bit as wild and loving and uncontrollable. In other words, exactly like I'd imagined.

Although I swear I've never forgotten about a kid until I was halfway across the Atlantic. At least not yet. There's still time.

FOUR

You Never Pack the Stuff You'll *Really* Need at the Hospital

Nat

Okay, ladies, listen up. Some of you have already had your baby—or babies. You know the drill. You've got the war story. You've experienced the many wonders and swearwords that childbirth can bring. The rest of you are either getting close or thinking about taking the plunge. This chapter is for you. You're going to want to pay attention to this one.

First I am going to tell you what I packed in the bag that I brought to the hospital when I had my first baby. And then I'm going to tell you what I should have brought. Because, believe me: It's a *completely* different list of stuff.

This is actually how our Mom Truth videos got started, by the way. "Someone has to be honest with moms about what they need at the hospital," we said. And then we realized someone also needed to be honest with moms about everything else, too!

So what was in my bag? It's pretty embarrassing, now that I think back on it.

Lip gloss. Apparently I thought having a baby would be like going on a date and I'd be just dolling up my face looking all cute while a baby rolled out from inside me. Spoiler alert: I never used the lip gloss. Not once. My lips could have fallen off and I don't think I would have even noticed. Or cared. Bye-bye, lips, it was good while it lasted.

Evian water spray. You know, so I could enjoy a refreshing spritz while screaming my lungs out, sweating like a pig, and strangling my husband for knocking me up in the first place. So dainty.

Mints—two tins of them! Because I was worried that my breath might smell a little bit rank. You know what? It probably did. I'm pretty sure it was friggin' awful. But I never ate a damn one of the mints. It's funny how you forget about little stuff like that when you're busy feeding your baby eight or twelve or sixteen times a day.

A book. Yes, a book! I never read books when I had whole weekends to myself with nothing to do. I guess I figured that this was the moment I was going to strike up a lifelong love of fiction. I figured wrong. I obviously imagined "giving birth" to be something like "going on a cruise." That said, this book wouldn't be bad at the hospital, but only because you can use it to throw at your husband for getting you pregnant in the first place.

My playlist. Before going to the hospital, I fiddled with the order of the songs I wanted to hear while I was in the last stages of labor. I've never listened to it. Sorry, Katy Perry—the mood just never seemed right to hear about you kissing that girl. It wouldn't have mattered anyway. No one would have been able to hear the songs over the sounds of my own grunting.

A robe. And I made sure it was not only functional but also stylish— you know, just in case we decided to have people in for drinks or something. Yup, you guessed it: never wore it.

Just to feel a little bit better about myself and my dumb decisions, I'll tell you about a woman I know. In her bag, she brought a blow dryer and a hair straightener. Was she giving birth or going to the prom? Needless to say, she didn't use either.

Let's get you prepared so you do better than I did. Here's what you really need to bring to the hospital.

Hair scrunchies. Bring a bunch of 'em. After you have your baby, you're going to want to put up your hair—and you're going to want to leave it like that for, say, two or three years. Honestly. You're a mom now, and being a mom means you've got zero time to primp and groom like before. The hair goes up. The hair stays up. Yes, after a while your husband may start giving you a look that says, "Uh, feel free to shower at any point." But here's the beauty about the scrunchie—*we* never have to actually see how bad it looks. You're a mom now, so you won't have time to look in a mirror until your kid is four.

Ice packs. You'll probably have a headache, but that's not what the ice pack is for. Think a little . . . lower. There's no easy way to tell you this: Your cooch is going to be swollen and pulsing. It's going to be red and it's going to be angry. And if you have the courage to take a look, it may very well be unrecognizable. It's going to look like it lost a bar fight, and then tripped down three flights of stairs. Take my word for it: You're going to want to ice that puppy.

Underwear. Are you a thong type of gal, like me? Or do you maybe prefer sexy briefs? Either way, you're going to want to put those back in the drawer. Instead, clear your mind and ask yourself this very important question: What would Grandma wear? Take a trip to the local department store and pick up a value pack of the kind of underwear that was last considered provocative back around the time of the steamboat. We're talking about undergarments that provide *maximum* coverage. There should be room enough in there to accommodate a family of four on a camping trip. And believe me: You are going to need the extra fabric if you're planning to pull those suckers up over your Mom pooch.

Here's an added bonus: If your husband sees you in this underwear, he won't bug you for sex for at least a year. Although he may expect you to make him some cookies and a nice bowl of soup, like his granny used to do.

Another reason you're going to want a sturdy pair of underwear is that there may be some activity down there. Some resettling of the foundation, if you know what I mean. I remember being told to bring along a panty liner or two because "there may be a little blood and fluid leakage." That poor panty liner didn't know what it was in for. Let's just say that it was a war zone down there, and the liner lost the battle.

A panty liner provides a delicate layer of protection. Screw delicate! This is a time for industrial-strength protection. I'm talking maxi pads. I'm talking *mega* pads! I'm talking two maxi-mega pads glued into the bottom of your granny panties. Stick another one on top. Stuff one more in there for good measure. You can't be too careful. You are going to be so soft and puffy in that region. The only person who could get turned on by you is the Michelin Man.

Laxatives. I feel like you can work this one out for yourself and you don't need any gruesome details from me. Although I will share with you that one day—superearly in the morning—I picked up my phone, and this is how Cat said hello: "Holy cow, my poops hurt!"

Hemorrhoid pillow. You're going to need one, okay? Not because you're going to get hemorrhoids (although you might—fun!) but because it hurts so friggin' much just to sit down. You need cushioning, girl! Send your man to buy a butt pillow before you even go to the hospital. Maybe it'll be a little awkward for him, and he'll be at the checkout going, "It's not for me! My butt is fine!"—but screw it, you're doing all of the work, so he can take one for the team.

In all seriousness, though, probably the most important thing—the *only* essential thing—to bring to the hospital is support. The source of that support is going to be different for everyone. It could be your spouse, a parent, a friend, a nice lady you rented on Craigslist. It doesn't matter. That's all you really need. Someone to talk to, to hear from, to confide in, to share with. Someone to yell at, someone to cry with. Someone who can run out and buy you some laxatives. You probably forgot to bring them.

FIVE

I Tried to Be a Cool Mom and I Almost Pooped Myself

The nurse came into my hospital room with a smile on her face and a clipboard in her hand. I was halfway out of my hospital gown before she finished speaking the sentence that I'd been so desperate to hear: "It's time to go home, Natalie."

I was excited. I was relieved. And, yeah, I was maybe just a little bit terrified. But most of all, I was determined to prove something to myself, to my husband, and to the world. I was determined to prove that I was still the same Natalie I'd always been.

From the moment I got pregnant, I had vowed to myself that I wasn't going to turn into some frail little flower just because I'd had a baby. No way. Not me. I was never going to become one of those women who seals herself into a bubble and cuts herself off from her friends. Not on your life. I was going to be like the moms I saw on a trip I took to Europe. Those moms didn't let a little inconvenience like a newborn baby stop them from getting dolled up and going out to dinner at a fancy restaurant at nine o'clock at night. Those ladies kicked ass. Those ladies were Cool Moms.

I was pumped to show that I could do it all. I could be a mother and a wife and a friend. I could keep all those balls in the air, no problem.

I got my first opportunity just a few days later. Mark's parents had flown in to meet their granddaughter. On the day they arrived, Mark's dad asked if we wanted to go out for a bite to eat instead of having dinner at home. "Hell, yeah," I said. "I'm starving." Mark was a little less sure. "Aren't you tired?" he asked. "Wouldn't you rather just stay home?" And I was, like, "Pfft. It's no biggie. Let's do this."

From the moment we walked in, I was the star of the restaurant. People kept coming over to get a look at Taylor.

"How old is your baby?" they'd ask.

"Just a few days," I'd reply, totally casually. (Cool Moms don't like to brag about their coolness.)

I ordered a plate of chicken wings, and Taylor slept like a champ. We all had a great time. I didn't feel tired or stressed. I was beaming. *Feel free to stop by our table and say hello, everyone. Feel free to come meet the city's newest Cool Mom.*

We left the restaurant and headed home. Traffic was pretty crazy, so it was taking a while. I dozed off in the backseat for a few minutes. But then suddenly, I was awake. I mean, I was *wide awake*. My body jolted me out of slumber for a very specific reason—something was happening to it. Or rather, something was inside it, if you know what I mean. A storm was brewing.

I'd never felt anything like this before, but I could tell that I had to act fast. At the same time, I wasn't exactly psyched to scream out in front of my in-laws: "I need to take a poop *really bad*!" Luckily, Mark picked up on the urgency of the situation and had his dad pull into the parking lot of a gelato place.

I tried to be casual about it. "Oh, I just need to pee. I'll only be a minute. No big deal." You know, stuff a Cool Mom would say. In truth, I was clenching every muscle in my body. Something was trying to get out of me. Actually, it felt like *everything* was trying to get out of me. I wish I had a video of me walking from the car to the door—I bet I looked like the Penguin in those old Batman movies. Waddle, waddle, waddle. I remember sweating from the effort of keeping my butt closed.

Anyway, spoiler: I made it into the stall. Barely. As for what happened next, I'm not sure how much detail you're comfortable with.

How about we do it this way? Go on and skip ahead to the next paragraph if you get queasy at the sight of blood. Skip now. Okay, have we gotten rid of the softies? Good. Because I'm here to tell you that I dropped the load of all loads into that poor, defenseless toilet bowl—everything short of my uterus itself. It felt like I lost about eight pounds in three seconds, which sounds like a hell of a diet plan. But not one I'd ever want to try again.

Cat and I are not going to give you a lot of advice in this book. We've been doing this parenting thing for nine years and we're still pretty clueless. But I'm going to make an exception here. You're going to want to grab a pen and underline this next sentence, okay? Or maybe cut it out and use a magnet to stick it up on the fridge. Ready? Here we go.

A few days after giving birth, your body is not ready for friggin' chicken wings.

After an experience like that, most women would probably get the hint. Take it easy. Don't try to be a hero. Maybe have a salad instead of two pounds of deep-fried meat.

But the siren song of the Cool Mom was just so much louder.

A couple weeks after I had Taylor, it was New Year's Eve. We'd been invited to a big party at a friend's house, but Mark suggested we stay in. We were both completely bagged. Neither of us was sleeping well. In my head, I thought, "Oh, wow, that sounds perfect. Let's stay in and go to bed early." But what I said out loud was "Screw that! We're going to the party!"

God, I am so stubborn. Somehow there was still a part of me that insisted on proving I could do it all—despite the unforgettable horrors of the Night of the Chicken Wings.

The first sign that going out was a bad idea? We got in the car and Mark drove to the *completely* wrong part of town, even though we'd known these friends for years. His brain just wasn't working. Neither was mine, apparently, because it took me about fifteen minutes to ask why he was going the wrong way. Naturally, we blamed each other and screamed at one another for a while. Not a great omen for a killer New Year's.

The second sign that this was a bad idea was also the final sign. We showed up at the party. We started chatting with some old friends. And within half an hour I was bawling my eyes out for no apparent reason. I just lost it. Everything caught up with me, I guess. The emotions were overwhelming and uncontrollable. I'm sure some of the people at the party thought to themselves, "I had no idea an escaped mental patient would be joining us tonight." It was a real shitshow. We hustled out the door, drove back home, and turned on the TV just as the ball was dropping in Times Square.

As we sat on the couch, I remember thinking to myself: A new year lies ahead! A year of waking up four times a night and spending whole entire days covered in puke! A year of not being able to control my emotions! A year of breaking down and crying in front of friends and strangers alike!

And that exact moment is when I made my decision: No more trying to have it all. No more trying to impress people with my Cool Mom moves. No more taking Taylor to fancy restaurants. No more parties. None of it—at least not for a little while. I don't need to prove I'm a hero. I'm a mother. I already proved it.

Oh, and no more chicken wings. Not for a little while, at least.

SIX

Um, There Are Going to Be Some Awkward Cooch Moments

I stood in the bathroom with my yoga pants on the floor and a mirror in my hand. I'd been home from the hospital for a week, and I hadn't been able to find the nerve to do it. But I could still hear the words of my doctor ringing in my ear. He had been very clear as I was leaving. Once every few days, I was supposed to take a moment out of my busy morning, find a bit of privacy, and . . . take a close-up gander at my cooch.

My privates had been through a lot in the delivery. They'd been torn up and stitched together. The doctor said it was superimportant to keep an eye out for infection. *You don't have to tell me twice, Doc. This girl does* not *want to deal with a cooch infection.* But here's the problem: I *cannot* look at stitches. Can't do it. It makes me feel sick even to *think* about looking at stitches. Beyond that, I was overcome by the fear of what I might see. It was bad enough that I had to *feel* what went on down there. I didn't want to have to look at the aftermath, too.

I put the mirror back in the drawer and leaned up against the counter. I was in a bind. What's a new mom with fifty stitches in her vagina supposed to do? I thought it through.

"Marc, babe, could you come in here?" I shouted.

My hubby was in for a surprise.

*

The first time I ever saw my husband, he was sitting across a bar from me. I was having a drink with a friend and absently scanning the place as she talked. My eyes locked on this superhandsome dude. I remember this part like it was yesterday. I actually interrupted my friend (rude, I know) and said out loud, "Oh my God, check out that guy. He's dreamy." Yes, I actually used the word "dreamy," like a character in *Grease* or something. It might have been love at first sight. It was *definitely* lust at first sight.

I don't know if you're getting a sense yet of the kind of person I am, but I'm not the type to wait for something good to happen to me. People miss out on opportunities every day because they're scared or because they're too busy staring at their phones. I got my ass off that barstool. I wandered over and introduced myself. I was confident. I was charming. I was a hot blonde in my early twenties. We looked into each other's eyes, and as the music played . . . he looked away. Dreamy Dude wanted nothing to do with me.

I later found out why. Turns out he was a hockey player, and not just the kind that plays in the Thursday night beer leagues. Marc had made it into the professional ranks, which is superhard in a country like Canada, where hockey is basically a religion. He had spent the past decade living all across Canada and the United States. On the night I saw him across the bar from me, he was in Toronto. He took one look at this tipsy blonde making a beeline toward him from the other side of the room—and he immediately thought: puck bunny. He figured I was a groupie. He thought I made a career of making it with hockey players. He blew me off. I didn't even get his number.

A few months later, I showed up for a blind date—and guess who's sitting at the table waiting for me? Dreamy Dude. Mr. Cold Shoulder. He had no memory of me, of course (so many puck bunnies, so little time)–but I *definitely* remembered him. After all, I'd spent a whole week thinking about what he might look like with his shirt off. We had a great time that night. At least I think we did.

Marc was in training, so he wasn't drinking. I, on the other hand, drank like a fish, because I'm classy like that. We talked about the coincidental nature of our second meeting. Maybe the universe was trying to tell us something.

A week later, I bumped into Marc at a corner store in my neighborhood. Turns out it was his neighborhood, too. He'd been my neighbor the whole time. Okay, universe, we get it already! You're not being very subtle.

*

Marc walked into the bathroom slowly, sensing that this might be a trap. I can't remember exactly how I raised the subject. I'm pretty blunt, so I probably said, "Time to check out my war wound, babe?"

That said, I didn't want to traumatize the guy. I'd read about men who'd watched their babies being delivered—and then could never quite look at their wives the same way, on account of what they'd seen down there. Men have a very clear idea of what a woman's vagina is supposed to look like. They've been staring at them in magazines and online since they were eight. They've been thinking about them roughly every twelve seconds of every dang day. For some guys, seeing it in the context of the birthing process or—in my case—having to look at it when it's all beat up . . . that's probably going to come as a shock.

So before sending him on his mission, I was, like, "You're okay with this, right? You're going to look at me the same and you're still going to think I'm hot and everything, right?" Marc just laughed. "Yeah, we're good," he said. But I had to be sure. I grabbed him by the shoulder. "No, you're *really* okay with this, right? You know that I just had a baby, so it's not going to be picturesque down there."

I should have known that part wouldn't bother Marc. During his hockey career, he was not afraid to get a little physical with the guys on the other team. Sometimes that meant checking them hard into the boards. Other times it meant punching them in the face, and getting punched back in the face for his troubles. One season, Marc managed to get 264 penalty minutes—the most on his team. Bottom line: He was pretty intimately familiar with stitches. He'd been sewn up a bunch of times.

"I got this," he said, and he dropped to his knees.

*

It's not easy having a relationship with a hockey player. He's never in town for more than a few days at a time. He calls or texts from random places you've never heard of. And he's almost always sore, which is a great excuse for getting out of doing a lot of the things that your girlfriend wants to do.

Six years after that blind date, as Marc's career was winding down, he asked me to go snowshoeing on a beautiful winter morning in Muskoka, a cottage and vacation area north of Toronto. Our bulldog, Wendel (named after a hockey player, obviously), was with us, plowing through the snow and having a blast. At one point, I looked back and saw that I'd taken a pretty healthy lead on Marc. Not that it was a race—but if it *was* a race, I was totally kicking the ass of a professional athlete. I started pushing the pace even harder.

That's when Wendel came bounding up from behind. As he ran

by, I noticed a glint of something on his collar. What was that? Was that . . . *Was that a ring?* I lunged and reached out. I caught Wendel's collar by the thumb and forefinger. At which point the collar snapped off! The ring—yep, I could see it now; it was a diamond ring—went flying into the air. I can still see it in my mind . . . rising slowly into the air, gently falling down . . . so close to my outstretched hand . . . and then landing in two feet of snow.

I need you to picture this next part, so you can see it as I remember it. On a sunny winter morning, amid a charming stretch of pine trees heavy with overnight snow, a man and a woman are on their knees—frantically digging through a drift in search of an engagement ring that, until recently, was attached to a dog for some reason. The man is calm and laughing. The woman is cursing like a sailor. I mean, the f-bombs are dropping by the dozens. She is frantic. At which point the dog circles back to see what all the fuss is about— and immediately starts humping the woman. I mean, *really* going to town on her. Yeah. So long story short, my engagement story is: profanity and canine thrusting.

The snows eventually parted, and we found the ring, just when I was about ready to take a flamethrower to the entire field. On the long trek back to the cottage, it occurred to Marc that he'd forgotten to do something. "Oh," he said, "will you marry me?"

*

I looked down at the top of my husband's head as he inspected my vagina. I have a very clear memory of thinking, "Now *this* is exactly the kind of thing they never warn you about in those baby books."

It never seems to come up in marriage vows, either. You don't hear many men vowing to love, honor, and examine your vaheen for postpartum infection.

After a quick look, Marc popped back up with a smile on this face. "All good," he said. "Everything's healing up nice." To him, it was a quick and funny moment in the bathroom—an impromptu check-in with his wife's privates. He probably didn't think about it again. But I was grateful for what he'd done. It was one less thing to worry about, at a time in my life when I was worried pretty much 24/7.

The next few months would be hard—superhard. Our relationship would get very strained as he worked long hours and I stressed over the baby. We would struggle to adapt. I would get angry at him. He would get frustrated with me. But at that moment, as he walked out of the bathroom, I'd never been more in love with him. I actually whispered these words to myself after he'd gone. I said, "Thank God he's him."

SEVEN

"Hey, in case you're not gay . . ." or, How I Met My Husband

Nat

I gave my cousin a nudge and gestured toward the front of the restaurant. Two men sat at the table by the window. They were drinking beer and chatting quietly. I didn't care what they were talking about. But as a twenty-five-year-old single woman, I was definitely clued in to the fact that one of them was smokin' hot. "Think those guys are gay?" I whispered.

It had been a long day. My parents, my cousin, a friend, and I had spent much of the afternoon at a family baptism in a town near Quebec City. We were having a quick dinner in Montreal before heading to a hotel. The restaurant was an upscale place—Dad was picking up the tab. It was a Sunday night. Not the usual recipe for a buddies' night out, right? "They have to be gay," I said, mostly to myself. Of course, that didn't stop me from glancing over there roughly two hundred times. There may also have been a hair flip or three. Ladies, I am not exactly the queen of subtlety.

Shortly after our entrées arrived, the two men stood to leave. I felt a surge of panic. What should I do? In my mind, I imagined racing across the restaurant, flinging tables and chairs out of the way, and hollering, "Please be straight and single, you beautiful man!" In reality, I settled on a slightly less pathetic approach. As he turned toward the door, Mr. Possibly French Hot Guy glanced our way. And that's when I hit him with it. That's when I hit him with a look. Not just *a* look—*the* Look. I summoned all my feminine wiles and gave him a sexy, sultry look that said, "Hey, in case you're *not* gay . . ."

He saw my look. He saw the Look. He *felt* the Look.

And then he left.

Fuck.

My cousin and my friend had a good, long (possibly too long) laugh at my expense. The Look had failed to work its magic. "He's definitely gay," I said, trying to salvage some pride.

Five minutes passed. Then ten. We were moving on to dessert when the restaurant door opened. Two men walked in. They were back. *He* was back.

He had seen the Look—and he'd made the decision to return. I smiled as he approached our table. He smiled back.

His name was Mark. I'm sure his friend had a name, too, but I didn't care what it was. My entire brain was consumed with the important task of examining every square inch of Mark's body. After my parents left for the hotel, the guys bought some drinks. They took us dancing. It got sweaty, and Mark removed his blue button-down. I can still picture him standing in his white T-shirt. I can still feel the feeling that I felt at that moment. I thought to myself, "I am going to marry this guy."

Mark was an American who lived in Boston. He and his friend were visiting Montreal because they'd never been to Canada before, and they had nothing to do that weekend. It was a total fluke that they were in town. It was a total fluke that *we* were in town. Or was it? I've always placed a lot of faith in fate. I'm a big believer that if you put something out there into the universe—a hope, a dream—it will come true. I make wishes when I blow out birthday candles, when I see the night's first star, and every time I drive over train tracks (I may have invented that one).

I'm also sappy enough to believe in love at first sight. Since I was a teenager, I don't think I've ever felt attracted to a guy without also wondering: Is he the one?

My friends in high school called me boy crazy. So did my parents, actually. I dreamed of finding a man, getting married, and having a family. I know that's a bit of a cliché, but it's true. At the time I met Mark, I had a well-worn issue of *Weddingbells* magazine next to my bed. I'd cut out the photo of the gown I planned to wear one day. And I'd marked the page that featured the most amazing engagement ring I'd ever seen.

I spent the entire drive home from Montreal composing a message in my head. I had made a decision: I was going to walk up to my room, turn on my computer, and type an email that basically said, "Hi, Mark, I am already deeply in love with you. You are the one." I was nervous. I knew this was a big move that could backfire. My hands were shaking as I clicked open my email.

There was a surprise waiting for me—a message from Mark. I literally gasped, which is a weird thing to do when you're alone. I swallowed hard and opened the email. I couldn't believe it! His message said all the things that I was going to say to him.

Eighteen months after that night in Montreal, Mark proposed to me on a small island off Cape Cod. We traveled there by boat in the early morning to watch the sunrise. He packed breakfast. As we reached the shore, he put one knee down in the sand, lifted a ring box, and asked me to marry him. I said yes even before he'd opened the box. I said yes even louder once I saw what was inside.

The first time Mark came to Toronto to visit, I'd shown him the photo of that amazing ring in *Weddingbells*. Without me knowing, he had later ripped out the page—and had a ring made to look *exactly* like the one I'd always wanted. Perfect, right? Everything was perfect.

A few years later, I looked into the eyes of this amazing man—this man I wanted to knock over furniture to get my hands on; this man I married with a giddy grin on my face—and thought to myself, "He doesn't get me at all." The arrival of our first daughter had strained our relationship. Everything had changed. Nothing was perfect.

When we were planning this book, I said to Cat that it would probably be *way* better if our husbands were a couple of deadbeats who rolled in each night expecting dinner on the table and then rolled out for beers with the boys. That way, we'd be doing 100 percent of the parenting—and we could take 100 percent of the credit. In truth, our husbands are pretty awesome. They both kill it in the Dad department. They handle all seven kids with ease and good humor. They play with the children. They clean up and do the boring chores of parenthood. They are good people and good role models.

But here's the important thing: Even with this great, supportive guy, I went through a *really* tough patch after Taylor was born. I was in a dark place. Mark and I weren't communicating—we just didn't know how to adapt to our new reality. I can remember panicking that I'd have nothing to say to him when he got home from work because nothing—literally nothing—had happened since he walked out the door in the morning. I had no stories to tell. I had no new information to share. I had no new words to say. I had done the same thing I'd done the previous day, the previous week, the previous month.

It was so stressful. I never doubted our relationship. I still felt love for him. But there was this huge and weird distance between us. Sometimes an entire day would pass and we'd say only a few words to each other.

Even if your husband is understanding, that doesn't mean he understands. How can he? He can't truly know the ordeal of childbirth. I mean, what did he even contribute? He got his rocks off, did nothing for nine months, and then sat next to you in the delivery room and said nice but completely unhelpful things like "Push!" or "You can do this!" Nice job, big guy—you're a real hero.

From the conversations I've had with my friends, I'm pretty sure that a huge percentage of women spend half their time in labor wanting to strangle their husbands. Partly for getting us into this mess, and partly because we are reminded every few seconds how much pain we are going through while they chat up the nurse or sip a coffee and look at their phones.

As much as your husband might try (and not all guys even try), he can't understand how it feels in the days, weeks, and months that follow the delivery. He can't understand what it's like for your own body to feel like it's not your own. The strange sounds it makes. The new and extremely bizarre sensation of stuff leaking out of your breasts and . . . elsewhere. The fact that parts of you feel—and this is going to sound odd—out of place. Nine months before, your body was hot and tight. Now you're big and soft and lumpy. You're swollen in weird places, like your feet. *Sorry, babe—I'd love to go outside but I can't fit into any of my shoes anymore!* It's not that you hate how you look. It just confuses you. You look in the mirror and you're, like, "Wait, is that my face? My face doesn't look like that." It's all very natural. It's all completely normal for your body to feel this way. But it can be so hard to get used to.

Your husband also can't understand what it's like for your mind to switch into Mom brain mode. Yes, of course, you are both parents to this new little bundle of joy and shrieking. But only one of you physically brought this baby into the world. Only one of you can feed it with your own body. Here's how I'd describe the feeling of having your first baby: It's like no one else matters. Maybe you've always been the kind of person who makes dinner for your husband. Better open a can of beans, big boy. The baby isn't just your first priority—it's your only priority.

Mark tried. He would say things that, to him, sounded normal and helpful, like "Are you hormonal?" He was just trying to figure out why his wife was suddenly a crazy person, I guess. But questions like that only made me want to slap him.

It's not like I was easy to deal with, by the way. I would often ask for Mark's help—like I'd ask him to change a diaper or put new sheets in the crib. And then most of the time I'd get pissed off at *how* he did it. I was always telling him, "You're doing it wrong" or "That's not how I want it." So basically I wanted him to offer to help. I wanted him to *want* to help. And then I wouldn't let him help. Yeah, living with me can be tough. (Not that Cat is a breeze, either. For a recent birthday, her husband gave her the gift of a trip to Paris. Awesome, right? To which Cat replied: "That's very cute, but Paris is not my thing. I'm not going to sit in a café and drink wine. I have no interest in museums. Let's go to Vegas!" So, long story short, they went to Vegas. That's life with Cat, everybody!)

I am happy (and relieved) to say that Mark and I eventually worked our way out of it. We found a new normal. As our kids have grown, I have come to appreciate Mark's terrific way with the children—and the depth of the love he has for our family. But I've also noticed something about dads in general—something I kind of admire. They are simply not programmed to feel parenting guilt of any kind.

Most moms feel guilty about everything. Literally. *Everything*. But has anyone ever heard a dad talk about feeling guilty about something he did or didn't do as a parent? Has anyone ever met a dad who compares himself to other fathers? ("Steve did a better job of teaching his kid to throw a curveball than I did," said no dad ever.)

Dads don't waste their time and energy. They don't worry about what the dad next door is doing or not doing. They just live their lives and make their own decisions, oblivious to most things around them. Sometimes, that can be annoying. But I have to admit it: They've got the right attitude. There are times when Cat and I stop and ask ourselves: What would a dad do? Not always, though, because if we were like dads all the time, then the kids would never get dressed. Or bathed. Or fed. Or . . .

My relationship with my husband was changed by children. Yours may be, too. I'm not going to sugarcoat it: It was a tough slog. For a long time, I felt isolated and alone and more than a little bit jealous that he got to leave the house each morning and I didn't. There was no magic moment that brought us closer together. I don't have a surefire list of "tips" for you to follow like a road map. For us, it just took time. It was like we were acclimating to our new environment, like climbers or divers. We had to let our minds and bodies adapt to our new reality.

We finally got back to a good place—a *different* place, but a good place. We're part of a family now, and so much more than a couple. But every so often, just for old times' sake, just because I'll never forget that night at the restaurant and that sweaty white T-shirt, I still give him the Look.

LISTEN, YOU MAY NOT WANT TO HAVE SEX AGAIN RIGHT AWAY . . . OR, LIKE, EVER

C: Okay, so this chapter is going to be a little different. There are a few Mom Truths that we *both* need to weigh in on. So we're going to sit down together and talk them out.

N: And you're invited! Grab a glass of wine, join us here on the sofa, and let's talk about . . . sex. That's right: postbaby sex, y'all!

C: And let's get something out of the way right off the bat. This is important, okay? We know that there are moms out there who love sex. *Loooove* it. Can't get enough of the nasty. And they can't wait to get back at it after they give birth.

N: Still got them urges in their privates!

C: Settle down, Nat. Anyway, maybe you're one of those moms. Maybe you have your baby and immediately start counting down the days till you can get back to getting it on. More power to you, girl! But here's the thing: That is *so* not us. We are roughly one thousand percent the opposite.

N: So, yeah, Cat is not good at math. But do you want to know how great a friend she is? Tell them the nicest thing you ever did for me.

C: Nat had just had her second kid. We were having dinner, and the topic turned to sex because there were guys there, so of course it did. And Nat's husband, Mark, was asking, like, "How long do we have to wait until we can have sex again?" And most doctors and experts recommend six weeks or so, right? But before Nat could say anything, I blurted out: "Twelve weeks." And he just nodded. He totally bought it!

N: We were in such a fog after having our first kid that he obviously forgot how long we'd waited the first time.

C: Nat and I were staring at each other and she was literally in tears from trying not to laugh.

N: The best part is that when I finally let him in after about ten weeks, he was, like, "What a champ!" He thought I was being all heroic by going ahead of schedule.

C: So I gave her the gift of four beautiful weeks without a hard penis pressing up against her in bed. You can't put a price on that.

 N: For us, at this stage of our lives, sex is something we have just to get it done. It's not something we look forward to—it's more like going to the gym. It's an item on your to-do list.

C: Oh my God, that is so true. I can remember psyching myself up in the morning. "Okay, I've got to do it tonight! Tonight's the night! I can't let it go another day." Because the tension is there, and your guy is in a lousy mood because he's not getting any.

N: You just want to put the check mark next to it and know you're in the clear for a few days.

C: The first time I had sex after our first kid, I basically spent ten minutes telling Marc, "This isn't for fun. This is just to see if everything down there still works. I'm just going to lie here. Neither of us is going to enjoy this."

N: **Wow, you're really great at foreplay. You should totally write a book on foreplay called *Neither of Us Is Going to Enjoy This*.**

C: But it's scary at first, right? There's no passion. There's no desire. There's just . . . concern. It's, like, "Wait, something recently came out of there and you want to put something *in*?"

N: **I remember feeling like such a terrible person when I had no interest in sex even months after having Taylor. I felt like I was broken or a loser or something. But then I started talking to other moms about it and they were, like, "Dude, I'm the same." I thought I was the only one. It felt good to know I wasn't alone.**

C: Turns out having a nine-pound human come shooting out of your cooch can put the kibosh on your sex drive.

N: **Especially when it's followed by about a thousand nights of sleep deprivation and cabin fever.**

C: And oh, also maybe the delivery left you with some damage down there and every time you sit on the toilet you're worried that some important part of you is going to fall out.

N: **But the problem is that none of this affects the male sex drive. After our first baby was born, I felt that Mark was looking at me the same way as before. He still thought I was hot. Naturally. But what he didn't get was that as the woman, as the new mother, to me *nothing* felt the same.**

C: Your body looks different. It feels different, inside and out. There's milk shooting out of your boobs and they hurt all the time.

> *N:* **Those breasts aren't for you anymore, hubby! You're no longer first in line.**

C: Nothing changes for men. Literally, nothing changes. And everything changes for you. They can't grasp that because they can't feel it themselves.

> *N:* **I remember wanting so bad for my husband to understand what I was going through. I wanted him to understand how consumed I was by this little, new person. But it's hard to connect like you used to when you had time to go to brunch for three hours.**

C: You *want* your guy to connect with you—but the truth is he can't connect right now because you're not emotionally available to him.

> *N:* **Maybe this is just me, but I think that, as a mom, you kind of want to punish your husband for not being able to understand what you're going through. It's, like, "Sorry, guys, but we are *so* not focused on you right now." So get that boner away from me. And keep it away.**

C: Having a baby takes a flashlight and shines it on every crack in your relationship. And if there are no big cracks, it creates one. All of a sudden you have to find your way together with a whole new person in your lives. The entire dynamic of your relationship changes literally overnight.

N: And some guys can't handle it. They go into denial. Like, Mark actually said to me one time: "I know we have a kid now, but I just want the girl I had before."

C: Which is sweet, but also a little stupid, right? Open your eyes— that girl is gone and those days are over, Mark! Guys aren't that great at taking a hint. Somehow, despite all the evidence, they wake up in the morning and continue to live under the delusion that we are going to bang them at the drop of a hat.

N: It's, like, you can't even touch them without them thinking it's an invitation for sex.

C: You brush by him in the kitchen—your bodies *barely* touch—and some part of his brain interprets this as a signal. It's go time! Two seconds later he's coming up from behind you at the sink and trying to cop a feel. And I'm, like, "Dude, no, I was just trying to get the bowl, okay?"

N: Or you're bent over sweeping up the kitchen floor and, boom, he's grabbing your ass. And in your mind you're, like, "Is this idiot really doing this? Is he really so dense that he thinks that I'm going to pull down my yoga pants and we're going to get into it on this pile of dirt and old apple slices?"

C: Or maybe you put your head on his shoulder—just looking for a tender moment at the end of a ridiculously long day. And suddenly his hands are on your boobs.

 N: Subtle, right? After months of this, you find yourself taking precautions to avoid any situation that might lead him to think you're interested in sex.

C: You can't be too careful.

N: **You can't even give him a peek. I basically have to put on a winter parka and snow pants when I leave the shower. If I'm in a towel and he sees me, he thinks it's an invitation.**

C: The absolute worst thing you can do is let him see that you've bought new underwear. Doesn't matter if it's a thong or a pair of Fruit of the Looms. Doesn't matter if you bought them at a lingerie store or at Costco. He thinks there's going to be a show tonight.

N: **Okay, so, time to get practical. Let's say that you're like us. Let's say your interest in sex is pretty close to zero right now. He's the hunter and you feel like the hunted. What do you do?**

C: We've got some tips, ladies. Some strategies to deny the bone in a way that doesn't cause any unnecessary conflicts or arguments.

N: **We've been fighting off penises for years now. It's time to go public with some of our most effective strategies. Look out, fellas!**

C: Here's one of my faves: Flip on the TV and find a show he likes. Or put on some sports. Sit and watch with him for a bit. Make sure he's interested. Make sure he's hooked. Then pretend you're going to the bathroom and never come back.

N: **By the time he figures it out, you're already asleep. Better luck tomorrow night, big guy!**

C: Or take it to the next level. Put a TV in the bedroom and start binge-watching a series together.

N: This one is supereffective because you get to go to bed together—which gives him hope and makes him happy.

C: But when you get to the end of the show, *you* control what happens next. First possibility: One of you fell asleep during the show. If one of you is asleep, there can be no sex. You're in the clear for another twenty-four hours. Second possibility: You suggest watching another episode. Then just keep repeating this until at least one of you falls asleep.

N: Love this one. The key is picking a dramatic show with lots of cliffhangers. He wants sex, but he also wants to know if the blond dragon lady is going to chop the head off of the hairy sword guy.

C: Here's another way to get out of sex: Fake being asleep.

N: Fake being asleep! It's an oldie but a goodie.

C: The big part of getting this one right is the breathing. It's got to seem like real "asleep breathing." You can't be too quiet or exaggerate it too much, or he'll know you're pretending.

 N: And you've got to commit to it, okay? He's a guy. He's horny. He's definitely going to try to "subtly" wake you up with a few noises and maybe a cough or something. You can maybe stir a little bit, but don't open your eyes! If you open your eyes, it's over.

C: We've got one more. And, ladies, it's a classic.

N: Works every time.

C: The ten-day period.

N: "Oh, bad news, babe—I've still got my period. Still flowing down there. No can do on the making out. Good night!"

C: Meanwhile your period was actually done five days ago—but how would he know? He can't, like, fact-check it, right?

N: He might get suspicious if he's good at math or superobservant. But he can't risk accusing you of lying. He knows that if he says you're faking your period, he's going to be on the couch for a week.

C: It's foolproof.

N: And then, if you're feeling ambitious, maybe you package the ten-day-period plan together with complaining about your period a few days *before* it arrives—and, honey, you've got two weeks in the clear.

C: Penis-free living, baby!

N: By the way, we should have told you this earlier, but you definitely should not be reading this book around your man. You don't want him getting a peek at the battle plan. If he asks what you're reading about, tell him it's a chapter on nutritional content in school lunches.

C: Trust us: He'll lose interest immediately.

N: By the way, we joke around about this stuff, but we also know that for some moms out there, this can be a huge issue in their relationships—and the source of a lot of stress. It's been a big issue for both of us, so we know.

C: It can be so hard, and some moms are with guys who are maybe not so understanding or patient.

N: In all seriousness, though: Give it time. And tell your guy that he needs to give it time, too. It's such a huge emotional and physical change. It's a complete change in how you live and how you sleep. So most guys will understand that it's going to be a process.

C: And don't beat yourself up over it. You can't force these kinds of feelings. You can't just wave a wand and, poof, "Horny!" Some crazy stuff went on down in your private area!

N: Yeah, there's no magic horny wand, ladies.

C: Every other couple out there who's just had a kid is going through the same stuff. They're trying to find their way. It's a different path for everyone, but it's always got some twists and turns.

 N: Don't think it means he's going to give up on you. Don't think it means you're going to split up. Although I do try to see it from the man's perspective sometimes. Not often, but sometimes. For some men, sex is how they feel validated. It's how they know we love them.

C: If you're having sex, then everything is great and nothing else matters. Budgets don't matter, messes don't matter. Nothing matters if he's getting laid.

> *N:* My guy still tries in the middle of the night. Despite the fact that I have never once agreed to have sex with him in the middle of the night, I come back to bed and he still tries.

C: Got to give him credit for persistence.

> *N:* No I don't! I've just been up changing a diaper or having a baby gnaw on my boob for twenty minutes. It's three o'clock in the morning. I've got maybe three hours until I've got to get up and start making breakfast and school lunches. And this guy wants to screw! No way, buddy. Mama needs some sleep.

C: We weren't always like this, by the way. Back before kids, I wouldn't mind at all if my guy woke me up at three in the morning because he was hot for me. That was great. I was down for that.

> *N:* Totally. That was back when they could touch us without getting slapped.

C: Or they could buy us lingerie and we'd actually love it. We'd want to try it on. We'd *rush* to try it on.

> *N:* But news flash, boys: I'm not superkeen to try on lingerie after launching a baby out into the world through my body. I'm just not going to feel sexy. Maybe you're into my new curves,

but I'm going to feel soft and weird. And that is *so* not a sexy feeling.

C: Yeah, what part of "leaky milky breasts" do you think is going to put me in the mood exactly? What part of being gassy and having headaches is going to make me want to strip down and get it on?

N: When I was younger, I was completely obsessed with those women's magazines that claimed to be able to teach you how to get better at sex and please your man. I wanted to be good at it! I wanted him coming back for more.

C: Yeah, those days are over. The guys can go please themselves, if you know what I mean. Maybe there will come a day, far in the future, when the kids are grown up enough and I am rested enough and I feel good enough about my body that I'll catch my second wind and I'll be right back into it.

N: Could happen! We could get back to dolling ourselves up, and shaving it all, and pruning it all, and maybe even actually having a shower—and then, "Hello, I am here to seduce you."

C: Maybe our brains will stop being on high alert for a crying baby or a child coming down the hallway and about to burst into our room. But until then, big boy, it's going to be: Wait for it. Wait even longer for it. Then get it in, get it out, and get back to sleep.

N: That's a great title for a sex tape I'd actually watch: *Get In, Get Out, Get Back to Sleep*.

C: It's really weird to think about the whole desire thing. You and your husband have to manage life. Bills, taxes, packing lunches, driving kids to their activities, about a squillion other things.

N: **You're basically running a company together.**

C: You're running a company together, and then you're supposed to get nasty on a turn of a dime. That just doesn't work for me. I don't work that way. Now, if you want to take me away somewhere warm and private and relaxing, and you want to book me a massage and take me out to a nice dinner, then maybe . . . just maybe . . . there might be a little surprise for you at the end of the night.

N: **Or maybe you'll go back to your room and pretend to be asleep.**

C: Yeah, you're right. That sounds way easier. I'll probably do that.

NINE

You Are Not the Only One Who Feels This Way

Nat

I'm going to tell you one of the first things that Cat and I bonded over. It's weird, so try not to judge us, okay? We both got unreasonably hostile when people would look at our new babies and then turn to us and say, "You must love her so much!"

It's a little hard to describe why this bothered us. Of course we loved our babies! *Of course we did.* But at the same time, we had a lot of other feelings going on deep inside. And maybe we didn't love every second of being a new mother. And maybe, just maybe, we didn't feel the magical connection that we expected to immediately feel with our babies. We loved them with all our hearts. But it also felt a little bit like we were at war with them—that we were engaged in a battle of wills. And we were losing.

Most people have the best of intentions when they say stuff like that to a new mom. Same goes for when they give advice. They're just trying to help, right? But here's the truth (at least, here's *my* truth): When you're some stranger and you start giving advice to a first-time mom with a newborn, she's going to think you're judging her. She's going to think what you're really saying is "You're doing it wrong, you dumb idiot." That's how I felt, at least.

The first time I went on a plane with Taylor, she put on a real show for everyone on board. Red face, full volume—just an unending symphony of shrieking. The smiling older woman sitting next to me kept giving me ideas to try. I didn't mind at first. I knew she probably just meant well. But after a few minutes and a dozen "suggestions," I'll be honest. I wanted to strangle her. Try this, try that, have your tried this? "Maybe take her socks off," the lady said at one point. "Her socks may be hurting her feet." I turned to her and gave her the glare of all glares. Long story short: The woman didn't say another word for the entire flight. She probably thought I was a bitch. I didn't care.

A big moment for me came when I was visiting with a cousin of mine, who had worked as a nanny for a bunch of families. She was a total pro with kids of all ages. Just a real natural. Taylor spent most of the afternoon howling. She was inconsolable. Nothing I did worked. Nothing stopped her from crying. I was thinking to myself, "Where is the mother's intuition I was supposed to get when I had my baby? Everyone talks about mother's intuition, but here's my little girl and I have no fucking clue about why she does anything she does."

Finally, my nerves were so shot that I just handed Taylor to my cousin. It was time to turn things over to an expert. "Why is she crying and why won't she stop?" I asked, point-blank. I was at the end of my rope.

Five minutes later, Taylor was still squealing. My cousin handed the baby back to me, shrugged, and said, "I have no clue why she's crying. She'll stop eventually." I'm not sure I can explain why those words mattered so much to me. For the first time, it occurred to me that maybe Taylor's crying wasn't my fault. Maybe I wasn't doing anything wrong. Maybe this is just how babies are sometimes. Maybe, just maybe, I'm not the only one going through this.

You are not the only one going through it, either. You are not alone.

TEN

Babies and Bosses: They Can Be the Same Kind of Annoying

A few years back, I read an article online about what it's like to work for a terrible boss—like someone who is just the absolute worst. Some of the stories were both awful and hilarious. Those poor people, having to deal with such hotheads and tyrants!

And then it hit me: I work for a hothead and a tyrant, too. His name is Max. He is three years old. Think I'm exaggerating? Think again, girlfriend. Here are ten ways that little kids and terrible bosses are alike:

1. They make you do *all* of the work. They do literally nothing, and you do absolutely everything. And they are *totally* fine with that arrangement.

2. You put in the time, energy, and effort just for them to go and steal the spotlight.

3. They never want to hear what you have to say. They only ever want to hear themselves.

4. They're always changing their minds and are never consistent.

5. You're constantly trying to please them, but it's never, ever enough.

6. You're always living in fear—afraid that they'll go off on you and have a tantrum in front of everybody.

7. They're often irritated and angry. And you never know why they're mad, if you did something to make them mad, or how to deal with them being mad.

8. When you're working with them, they're constantly micromanaging and telling you what to do and how to do it. I want it like *this*!

9. They never praise you, but they're the first to criticize you for doing something wrong.

10. They're self-centered. They're big-time liars. And they're rude all the time.

There's bad news and good news. The bad news: We can't quit our jobs as moms! The good news: Our little ones will eventually grow up, while the horrible bosses of the world probably won't.

CAT

ELEVEN

Instagram Is Bullshit

It's 10:15 on a Saturday morning and the sun is streaming in through the side window, hitting a patch of the playroom carpet where Chloe is playing alone with her little stuffed monkey. She looks absolutely adorable. I think about grabbing my phone and capturing this perfect moment to share with the world. But how perfect is it, really? Truth be told, there is a total gong show going on behind the scenes. Chloe's brother and sister are screaming at each other across the room. Marc is on the phone with the computer repair shop because one of the kids just spilled orange juice into our laptop. There are lines on my face from falling asleep on the couch when I was supposed to be at the gym.

Instagram is a great way of sharing images from your life. It's also a great way of making your life look a heck of a lot better than it is! And it creates a false expectation for new moms about what *their* experience should be.

Today's moms go to Instagram and Facebook, and what do they see? They see their friends and various celebrities who are also moms. Everyone looks like she's got it all together. Everyone seems like she's having the best time. And then you look up from your phone and your kids are howling, the kitchen is covered in cupcake batter, and you've got a giant ketchup stain on your third shirt of the morning.

Take a step back, ladies. Don't believe the hype! Here are ten of the biggest myths about motherhood that you'll find on Instagram:

Myth No. 1: Pregnancy is nothing but beautiful bliss. To judge from Instagram, the nine months of pregnancy are a time of leisurely brunches, thoughtful reflection, and caressing your belly over and over. My personal favorite is the artsy silhouette of a future mother as she strolls along a tranquil beach, the sun setting behind her ripened body. Everyone offers up deep quotes about the wonders of motherhood and the joys of growing a new human within. Weirdly, there's not a lot of mention of morning sickness or farting, or the fact that you have to pee every forty-five minutes, or the discomfort of trying to sleep with eight pounds of kid squirming around inside you. Instagram makes pregnancy look like a fairy tale. But we know better, right, ladies?

Myth No. 2: It's normal to be bikini-ready right after giving birth. Who are these women? How is this even possible? These women give birth and a month later they're standing in the waves with their newborns, wearing bikinis that I could barely have fit into in high school—let alone after three kids. How do they do it? Why aren't they wearing sweatpants and big, bulky absorbent pads like the rest of us? I think these women might be witches. Whatever the case, they set an impossible standard. A month after I gave birth to *my* first child, I was wearing so much Spanx when I went out in public that it took me ten minutes to go to the bathroom.

Myth No. 3: Moms love having coffee in bed with their kids. Instagram is all about the pursuit of the idyllic photo that suggests you are the perfect mom and you have the perfect children, and together you are leading perfect lives. What better way to show that than to snap a photo of you lounging in bed with a cappuccino as your loving children nap silently or obediently hang on your every word? One question: Are these kids sedated or what? Because in real life, they'd be either crawling all over you or jumping up and down on the bed like hyper monkeys. And your coffee would have long ago spilled over the perfectly crisp white pajamas you put on for your "spur of the moment" photo shoot. But we never see that photo, do we?

Myth No. 4: Each and every day after becoming parents, you fall more deeply in love with your partner. This is a classic. These photos are everywhere. Usually it's set up so that the woman's head is resting on the man's broad shoulder. The guy is gazing off into the distance with a peaceful look on his face—and the mom is glowing with contentment and wisdom as she stares down at their little baby. And then the caption is something like "More and more in love with each other, and our little one." Come on—you can be honest with us, lady. Sometimes, when you're stuck at home with the kids all day and Dad decides to go out "for a beer or two" instead of coming home, you sort of want to slap him in the back of the head, right? And why don't the two of you look cranky and exhausted in your photo? If you're going to post a pic where you look like models, you need to tell everyone how many nannies you have. It has to be at least three.

Myth No. 5: Everyone feels #blessed all the time. Nice try, Instagram moms, but we know you don't really spend each and every entire day in a state of perpetual gratitude. No one does. When your baby is up and howling at 2:45 a.m. for her third feeding of the night, you don't feel #blessed. If we were all a little more honest about the experience of motherhood, we'd see a lot more hashtags like #exhausted, #frustrated, and #bloated.

Myth No. 6: Your children will always be besties. Go ahead, moms. Post those sweet pics of the big brother kissing his new sister. Or the two toddlers playing together in cooperation and serenity. But why don't you do us all a favor and also post a photo from the same time the previous day, when the brother was biting the baby's ear and the one toddler had decked the other with a board book.

Myth No. 7: Kids are always dressed stylishly. It's weird. I live in a huge city, and in real life I hardly ever come across hipster babies wearing artfully distressed denim overalls, vintage Converse sneakers, and a plaid bonnet—and yet they seem to be everywhere on Instagram! Do some moms have access to a wardrobe department that I don't know about? And, hey, be sure to frame the photo so that you just happen to get your two-thousand-dollar stroller in the background.

Myth No. 8: Your house will always be clean. Guess what? Most parents don't have the time, energy, or domestic staff required to keep their kitchens looking like movie sets. But don't tell the moms of Instagram. Where do these people keep their stuff? Is it all just pushed off in a huge pile in one of the corners we can't see? Ladies, it's okay to have a toaster on your counter. We know you make toast.

Myth No. 9: Your kids will toddle off to school happily each morning. Some kids definitely will—because some kids love school. But it's odd how on Instagram you hardly ever see proud moms post videos of their sons sprinting away from school and trying to elude capture like animals in the wild—the way my son did for two years. And it's weird how you hardly ever see pics of their daughters crying loudly and literally trying to grab hold of the doorframe so they don't have to go to class—like my daughter did for far too long. Nope, in the world of Instagram, it's all cute backpacks and rubber rain boots. Meanwhile, I'm three blocks away from school trying to talk my son out of a tree.

Myth No. 10: Family vacations will be relaxing and heavenly. This is the biggest lie of them all. And the thing is, you don't even need to have a kid in order to know this. If you've ever flown on a plane, you've seen them coming down the aisle: the defeated mother carrying the shrieking child, followed by the sweaty father hauling fourteen bags over his shoulder with a look on his face that says: "I should have worn a condom." So relaxing! Then you finally make it to the resort, and your kids are playing happily on the beach—for ten minutes. Because young kids are only ever interested in doing *anything* for a maximum of ten minutes. So it's from the beach to the restaurant to the tuckshop to the pool to the gift shop to the kids' club and back to the beach. Congratulations—only nine more hours to go until dinner. So relaxing! But this much is for sure: All the Instagram pics are going to be of Mom and Dad wearing sunglasses and clinking cocktail glasses, and every hashtag is going to mention #paradise.

Nat and I do our best to show our "authentic" lives online—the good, the bad, and the up-all-night ugly. If you know us at all, you know we're not afraid to give you a big, long glimpse into what mothering *actually* looks like—the gross hair, the bags under our eyes, the whiny kids, the fighting siblings. In our world, the kitchen counter in the background of the photo isn't going to be sparkling clean and stylishly empty. It's going to be covered in mac and cheese. The sink is going to be filled with dishes. Craft supplies will be scattered all over the damn place. It'll look like we have seventy kids between us, not seven.

The perfect moms of Instagram always look so great and healthy. Their kids look happy and amazing. And I'm sitting on a sofa covered with toast crumbs, wearing the same yoga pants I've had on for three days, and *my* kids are all staring at screens. It can be hard. So it's important to remember that the truth of any photo is rarely what it seems.

I mean, think of it this way: You're scanning Instagram and you see this spectacular photo of a mother with her girls—and you're supposed to believe they just happened to be running in lace dresses at sunset in that apple orchard with the wind blowing through their perfectly coiffed hair? Riiiiight. All power to the mom for pulling together that amazing shot. The rest of us can appreciate it without judging ourselves against it. After all, we suspect that on her phone she probably has eighteen shots that didn't work out—before she finally got the one that did.

Nat and I still scroll through Instagram. We're never going to stop doing that! But when we come across a pic that makes us feel like we need to get our shit together, we stop for a moment and we imagine what happened the moment *after* the photo was posted. Maybe that adorable boy spilled ice cream on his expensive linen shirt. Maybe those cute, smiling girls started yanking on each other's pigtails. Maybe that gorgeous mom sharted a little bit.

Our guesses may be far from the truth. But then again, so were their photos.

TWELVE

My Husband Attacked Germs Like He Was Some Sort of Hygiene Ninja

Nat

If you had come to our house to visit in the months after our first daughter was born, you would have been met on the front steps by my husband. Mark would have greeted you with a smile and the world's biggest bottle of Purell. It wouldn't have mattered who you were: You weren't getting through that door until he'd basically given you a bath in the stuff. Hands, arms, exposed skin of any kind—none of it escaped his paranoid eye. It didn't take long for our friends to give Mark a new nickname. They called him the Sanitizer.

Mark took it as a compliment. He was obsessed with making our home a germ-free zone. We both were. We were overtaken by a primal urge to go to absurd lengths to protect our baby. We would double-sterilize bottles and nipples—just in case one hardy germ survived the first cycle in the dishwasher. Every Binky got boiled within an inch of its life. If it got dropped on the floor, we freaked out and raised the alert level to Binky DEFCON 1. The soother would be taken out of circulation until all germs had been annihilated to the Sanitizer's satisfaction.

If you had a cold, or had a cold two weeks ago, or felt like you might be getting a cold, or knew someone who once had a cold (even if that person lived on the other side of the country) . . . well, thanks for dropping by, but you were not getting into the house. No way. If you so much as cleared your throat within twenty feet of our child, you'd get a glare. Was that a cough? Were you sick? Thanks for visiting, but you were no longer welcome within the Fortress of Purell! I remember one time I leapt off the couch to stop a friend from handing a new stuffed animal to Taylor. What if it had germs on it? Or, like, the Ebola virus? What if it gave her allergies or a rash? Mark and I were like germ ninjas—always ready to pounce from the shadows and stop an approaching virus in its tracks.

I think most moms and dads can relate to that impulse. It's about trying to seal out the world. We want to do everything we can to protect our little babies. In our case, that meant basically making our house as sterile as an operating room. What's that? You want to hold our little Taylor? Well, go put on this hazmat suit and then sign this letter promising not to exhale in her general vicinity.

It wasn't just us—and it wasn't just inside our house. Cat and I used to keep our walks short because we didn't want to expose our little ones to air pollution. We'd tense up every time a truck drove past—and we'd turn away from the clouds of exhaust fumes. We'd try to keep our babies away from loud noises, too. Everywhere we looked, we saw a threat. Is that guy smoking? Are those lights too bright?

Now let's jump ahead to a year ago. We were at the local hockey rink, watching a game. Our three-year-old, TJ, wandered off—TJ wanders off roughly three hundred times a day, it's his favorite thing to do—and eventually I started scanning around the rink to try to spot him. That's when I heard him. He was below us, hanging out under the bleachers. A typical kid thing to do. I bent over and peered down, and here's what I saw: Our precious little TJ was trying to remove a hunk of used gum from the bottom of a bench. Gross, right? Hang on. It gets worse. He was trying to get it off using . . . *his teeth*.

Yep, you heard me. Mouth open, gnawing away at a hardened wad that could have been left there at any time by anybody with any kind of weird mouth issues. That gum could have been older than TJ. Heck, it could have been older than me!

A few years earlier, this would have triggered a panic attack of epic proportions. Mark would have grabbed the kid, fled the arena, and spent the next calendar month dabbing TJ's mouth with pretty much any product that had the word "antibacterial" on its label. He would have been on the phone to the doctor. He would have been on the Internet searching "Are gum germs fatal?"

Luckily, there comes a point in the parenting cycle when even people like Mark loosen up and realize that the microscopic world may not be as grave a threat as once feared. For me, the turning point had come one morning at the grocery store. TJ was two years old and riding in the shopping cart. As he reached out to try to grab a box of Froot Loops, his Binky slipped away and fell to the floor. I glanced around quickly. There were other moms in the aisle, so I picked it up and put the Binky into my pocket. As soon as the coast was clear, I rubbed it off a bit and stuffed it back in TJ's mouth. He'd be fine, I thought. And he was fine. A lot had changed in a few years. When Taylor was young, I'd wash her sheets almost every day to ensure that not a single dust mite found its way to her skin. Today, if I caught TJ licking a squirrel, I'd be, like, "Ehh, it'll help him build up his immunities."

It's not just germs. Your standards start to slip in other areas, too. With your firstborn, you are supercareful about diet—when she starts on solids, what kinds of foods he snacks on, that sort of thing. But later on, you may not be so obsessive about it. In fact, you may begin to forget about that stuff entirely. One time, Cat was visiting with her stepsister, who had a son who was about to turn one. It was a hectic night, so Cat offered to feed the boy. She gave him a healthy dinner and, for dessert, a little chocolate sundae. Cute, right? The boy was covered in ice cream and happy as a clam when his mom walked back into the kitchen. Here's how the conversation went . . .

Stepsister: What the fuck are you doing?

Cat: What? He's never had ice cream?

Stepsister: He's never had *sugar.*

Cat: [*Long pause*] Oops.

We all know that kids go through phases—but so do parents. When our first baby is born, our default state is to be psychotically overprotective. We are hardwired to do anything and everything to keep this little helpless thing from being exposed to harm, or risk, or germs. And that's the way it should be. Babies are tiny and fragile.

It's good for our kids that we start with high standards. It's good for our own mental health—and theirs—that we learn to ease up. Kids need to be able to explore, to dig around, to get messy, to stick their hands where they shouldn't stick their hands.

Once you have a second kid, it becomes less of a priority. And once you send your kids to daycare or to school—forget about it. They are immediately exposed to the full spectrum of germs, contagions, cooties, and whatever else. They're sitting and playing all day in close quarters. If one kid's got something, they've all got it. They are going to come home sick. They are going to make other kids sick. They're going to have pinkeye for two weeks, hacking coughs for six weeks, and runny noses from roughly September to July.

You come to learn that there's nothing anyone can do about it. Not even the Sanitizer can protect them. But they'll be fine anyway.

THIRTEEN

All Those Hideous Clothes Aside, the Moms of the 1970s Had It Made!

As overstressed and underappreciated millennial moms, we sometimes wonder what our lives would have been like if we'd been parents in another era—when there were different ideas about what it meant to raise a child, and different views on how much was expected of a mother.

We bet that the 1970s would have been an awesome time to be a mom. Here are ten reasons why:

1. *Safety rules were, um, let's call them "flexible."* Today's moms spend hours researching the safest and most reliable car seat on the market. We break our backs making sure that the seat is properly and snugly installed. We scrunch into the backseat a zillion times a day to fasten and unfasten the straps and belts that keep our children safe. The seventies mom basically opened the door and let the kids hop in and bounce around in the backseat like loose cargo. No seatbelts, no judgment. You didn't have to hassle your kid to wear a helmet when he rode his bike, either. You just had to drive him to the hospital when he fell off and whacked his head. (He didn't have to wear a seatbelt on the way.)

2. *Staying slim was easy.* Moms didn't need to eat healthy or diet or work out every dang day to maintain a thin figure. They all shared an amazing hobby that kept them skinny—smoking! Sure, it might ultimately cause your premature death. But you didn't have to worry about carbs!

3. *Drinking was encouraged.* Cocktail hour wasn't a guilty pleasure. You didn't need an occasion or an excuse. It wasn't a weekend-only ritual. It was a daily household celebration. And it often lasted much longer than an hour!

4. *Meal prep often consisted of opening a can.* Forget about the pressure to make elaborate, healthy dinners. Forget about rushing to the supermarket and standing in a long line to buy fresh ingredients. Just grab the can opener and crack open that tin of Spam! Mmm . . . meat in a can.

5. *Your babysitter was any kid who was older than your kids.* Today's moms interview potential candidates. We ask for credentials and references and medical histories and criminal record checks. We do everything short of hooking them up to a lie detector. Here's how the process went back in the seventies: A mom would ask, "Is that teenage girl down the street in jail?" If the answer was no, boom, say hello to your new babysitter.

6. *Moms didn't know where their kids were 24/7.* No GPS. No texting or cell phones. The mothers of the 1970s let their kids roam the neighborhood with no supervision, knowing they'd return when the streetlights came on—or when their stomachs got hungry. If a seventies mom really needed her son for some reason, she'd just open the door, take a step outside, and holler his name across the neighborhood. Could you imagine if *you* did that? You'd get mocked in an online meme and probably arrested for child abandonment.

7. *Long, feathered hair!* Put down this book right this minute, pick up your phone, and Google "Farrah Fawcett-Majors." She was one of the most famous women of the 1970s—the star of *Charlie's Angels*. Literally every woman dreamed of having hair like hers. We know this has nothing to do with parenting, but *check out that amazing hair!* Yes, please.

8. *You could force your kid to walk over and change the TV channel.* In the age before the remote, someone had to get up from the couch and make the long trek to change the channel to *The Love Boat.* That person was *never* the mom. Manually changing the channel is why God invented children. Life was sweet for seventies moms!

9. *You didn't have to compare yourself with "perfect" Instagram moms.* The only mothers you ever saw were the ladies in your neighborhood, and from what we're told most of them were pretty committed to the curlers-and-housecoat look—even in the afternoon. A decent pair of sweatpants would have made us look high end!

10. *Mom shaming wasn't a thing.* Seriously—talk to *any* woman who raised children in the 1970s. Ask her if other moms judged how she brought up her kids, or if she ever criticized the parenting of other moms. She'll literally laugh in your face. Can you imagine? Nobody giving you that "look" when you show up to the bake sale with store-bought cupcakes. Nobody whispering behind your back when your kid rolls into school with his pants on backwards.

It sounds to us like seventies moms just lived life and had a good time. We could all learn something from that relaxed approach to parenting. Let's bring it back! Although maybe we'll skip the curlers-and-housecoats part of it.

FOURTEEN

Dads Are Pretty Clueless, So Let's Try to Help Them Help Us

CAT

Okay, Moms, we're going to get a little sneaky here, and we need your help. It's time to whip your husbands into shape. Except we can't let them know that we're doing it, or they'll never play along.

Men are great and everything (or so they keep telling us). But most of them aren't very good at picking up on subtle clues, or even on obvious clues. They have trouble reading between the lines of a woman's comments and determining how they should respond. Also, a few dads haven't quite figured out that something has changed in their relationships with their wives. (Fellas, here's a hint: It has something to do with that screaming baby in the crib!)

Anyway, I'm going to help train your husband for you. Here's all you need to do: Turn to the next page and then call out to your man. Say something like "Hey, honey bear, these pages of the book are for you!" Make sure you mention that it's only a couple pages. From our experience, that's about the most a man can read about parenting before getting bored and watching all eight Fast and Furious movies in a row.

Don't let him read this section where we point out that basically we're trying to trick him into being a better husband! Okay, here we go . . .

Dear husbands,

We know it can be difficult being a dad. I mean, sure, we moms carried the baby for nine months and gained all the weight and went through labor and delivered the baby and nursed the baby. But you remembered to bring pretzels to the delivery room. You're the real heroes.

Sometimes a new dad has so much on his plate (work, beers after work, hockey after beers after work) that he needs a little assistance understanding how to deal with his wife, now that she's also a mother.

I'm here to help. I'm here to show you how to decode what your wives are trying to tell you—and how you should respond. This last part is key! You really do have to respond. It's not always enough to nod vaguely while looking down at your phone.

Feel free to come back to this chapter as often as you need to. Come back every damn day if you want! It may take a little practice, but you can totally figure out what your wife is telling you. After all, you're the real heroes.

> **When she says:** "I don't have any clothes that fit."
> **You should:** Send her shopping.
> **You should not:** Offer to lend her some of <u>your</u> clothes.

> **When she says:** "I was up <u>all night</u> with the kids."
> **You should:** Tell her to go back to bed. Then take the kids out for a long walk and bring her home a coffee.
> **You should not:** Ask what's for breakfast.

> **When she says:** "It's been an unbelievably long day."
> **You should:** Leave work a little early to come home and take over.

You should not: *Talk about your own day and tell her how tired you are from the martini you had at lunch.*

When she says: *"The kids have been so terrible today."*
You should: *Tell her what a great job she's been doing—and how she inspires you with her patience and dedication.*
You should not: *Act surprised and say, "The kids are always so perfect with me!"*

When she says: *"I'm feeling really overwhelmed."*
You should: *Ask how you can help. And then listen to what she says! And then do something about it!*
You should not: *Say any of the following things: "What's wrong with you?" "Suck it up, buttercup!" or "Cool, I'll be home to help as soon as I finish my six-hour fantasy football draft."*

When she says: *"I just can't get the hang of being a mom."*
You should: *Understand that <u>whenever</u> she talks to you, it's a perfect opportunity for you to tell her what a great job she's doing and how lucky your kids are to have such a wonderful mother.*
You should not: *Claim that you are totally killing it as a dad.*

When she says: *"I haven't seen another human except for you and the kids in five whole days."*
You should: *Say the three magic words that every mother yearns to hear: "Girls'. Night. Out."*
You should not: *Go along on the girls' night out.*

When she says: *"I'm at the end of my rope with these kids."*
You should: *Pour her a bath and offer to put the kids to bed.*
You should not: *Drop the kids in the bath <u>with</u> her.*

When she says: "I just need to be held for a minute."
You should: Rub her back until she falls asleep.
You should not: Interpret this as foreplay and remove your pants.

When she says: "I am so fat and out of shape."
You should: Tell her that she's beautiful.
You should not: Agree.

Guys, it's pretty simple, actually. Your wife doesn't need a lot. Mostly, she just wants you to understand what she's going through. And she wants you to pitch in when she needs the help.

Oh, and she probably wants you to keep your pants on.

FIFTEEN

My Name Is Natalie and I Am an Addict (My Drug Is Amazon Prime)

Let's get one thing straight about my habit: I don't use Amazon for books. I don't use it for clothes. I use Amazon to buy pretty much any gadget or gizmo that's supposed to help me become a better mom. Or, to put it another way, to help me make mom-ing a little easier. It is my go-to solution for every single problem that comes up. Baby not feeding well from the bottle? Time to buy some new bottles. Baby not sleeping well? Time to buy that weird device I saw that mimics sounds of the womb. Every time I click, I believe with all my heart that the solution to my woes and anxiety will arrive at my door overnight.

How bad is my addiction? I bought a soother that comes with a built-in thermometer—because that's a brilliant idea, right? (I don't think I ever used it for the thermometer part.) I bought some weird stuffed, cube-shaped development toy that was supposed to make my baby a genius. (How? I have no clue. My kid mostly just stuffed parts of it into his mouth.) During one extended period of intense sleep deprivation, I convinced myself that what we needed—what Mark and I *needed more than anything in the entire world*—was a fancy new indoor baby swing that cost, like, five hundred dollars. Truth is, I would have paid *anything* for it. That swing was going to fix my baby, fix our days, and fix my life.

That's how you get as a mom. You're very vulnerable. You *want* to believe that you're only one magical product away from a day that's a little less crazy and a night that's a little more peaceful.

In those early months, I came to understand why some women simply fall apart at the seams. The first six weeks can be hell—especially if you're like me and you get into your own head, and you're constantly thinking, "This is *my* responsibility. She is my responsibility and I'm screwing it up. You're screwing it up, Nat." You feel it every time your baby cries. You feel it every time you can't figure out what's wrong with her. You feel it every time your baby is wailing in public and people are looking at you like "Hey, can you stop being a terrible mother for just a minute and make your baby be quiet?" You feel the heat of all those eyes staring at you and judging you. You actually start to sweat. And you don't know what to do to make the baby stop crying, because you've tried everything. You feel like a failure. You think, "There has to be something out there that can help."

I can still remember how excited I was when the swing arrived. This was going to change everything! This was going to fill my afternoons with beautiful silence! It was going to put my baby into a better mood because she'd be so well rested!

When Mark finally finished putting it together, we noticed that it basically took up half of the living room of the tiny apartment where we lived at the time. But that was a small sacrifice if it meant our baby would finally sleep. We placed Taylor into the seat. We attached the safety straps. We fired it up. And sure enough, five minutes later, we were looking at a sleeping, swinging daughter. Hooray! Best purchase ever!

Hours later—literally just hours!—a friend sent me a link to a video that basically said, "*Do not let your baby sleep in a swing!* If you let your baby sleep in a swing, she might never learn to fall asleep in a bed." I was crushed. Heartbroken. With an incredible amount of regret, I got rid of the five-hundred-dollar snooze machine that had taken over the living room. My dream of afternoon silence went unfulfilled.

Cat calls me an Amazon junkie. She says she can't spend an hour at my house without hearing the doorbell ring for a delivery. I remember I bought these things called Walking Wings—which let you help teach your baby to walk without you having to bend over all the time and totally wrench your back. Genius, right? Anyway, I got these things and loved them. Two days later, I saw an article online that said, "Hey, don't use Walking Wings because your kids' legs won't get strong enough if you're supporting them all the time." And that's the last our kids ever saw of the Walking Wings.

(By the way, I have literally no idea whether those articles were right about the swing or about the Walking Wings. No clue at all. Those could both be awesome products. But the Mom brain is so trained to be protective that I immediately bailed on my new products the second I heard anything negative. And then, of course, I went right back on Amazon.)

It can be such a compulsive obsession to try to "fix" the baby. When things are bad, that's how you see it: The baby is a problem and somewhere on the Internet is the solution. The perfect piece of advice. The perfect gadget. The one amazing thing that will solve the baby and get your life back to something approaching seminormal. It's three o'clock in the morning and you've got eighty-five tabs open on your browser: baby bottles, reviews of baby bottles, fast flow, slow flow, wide neck, glass and plastic, baby bottles that cause less gas, and on and on. And at that moment, at three o'clock in the morning, when you've just fed your baby and you're about thirty minutes from feeding her again, what you're doing makes sense to you. Because you're thinking: If I just find the right bottle, everything will be fine. My baby will be fine. I'll be fine. For two years, my closest relationship with any man (not including my husband, obvs) was with the UPS driver in our neighborhood. I saw that dude *a lot*.

Deep down, there is probably a part of me that realizes a baby is just going to be a baby—and there's not much anyone can do about it. But when you're the mother of a newborn, there is a good chance you will become just a little unhinged—and no unhinged person is ever going to listen to the rational part of her brain. That part of your brain may as well go on vacation for eight years after you have a kid. You won't have much use for it. Instead, you'll be at the mercy of the part of your brain that believes every product seems like a good product. Every gadget seems like *the* gadget.

With sleep and a little distance, I have come to understand that you can't just throw money at parenting challenges—and expect to solve them with the click of a button. I also realized that so many of the things we stress over as moms—cloth or disposable, breast versus bottle, sleep versus co-sleep—really don't matter all that much in the end. Children eventually learn to sleep through the night. They eventually graduate from bottles. They eventually stop pooping their pants. Would they have done so without all those gizmos from the Internet? Almost certainly.

But I'll be honest with you: Even now, when I get frustrated as a mother, when anxiety strikes at 3:00 a.m., I'm still tempted to roll over in bed, pick up my phone, and say hello once again to my good friend Amazon.

SIXTEEN

LEAVING YOUR KIDS IS HARD . . . AND GREAT . . . AND DIFFICULT . . . AND AMAZING . . . AND IMPOSSIBLE . . . BUT DID WE MENTION GREAT?

We now take you live inside a typical mom's brain as she gets closer to taking her first trip away from her children . . .

One week before the trip: "I can't wait to go. Get me out of here!"

Three days before: "Maybe I shouldn't go away. They'll miss me, I'll miss them. No, no . . . I'll go. It'll be good to go."

The night before: "I can't go. What if something happens? They're so cute. Why are they so cute? I love them so much. I'm canceling my trip."

Mid-getaway: "What kids?"

Mid-getaway + one day: "I can't wait to get home! Maybe I'll change to an earlier flight. I can't stand to be away from them for even one more night!"

One hour after getting home: "I need a vacation."

N: We know that the Mom brain is a very weird and chaotic place, right? It's always firing off these contradictory impulses that can make our lives very difficult and confusing. But the Mom brain goes *completely* off the rails when the time comes to plan a few days away from your kids.

 C: Oh my God—you literally count the seconds until you get a break. You can't wait. You imagine how great it's going to be. And then when you finally get your break—when you get away from the madhouse—you count the seconds until it's over. Stepping away from kids is haaaarrrdddd.

N: So hard. Even if it's just for a couple of hours.

C: One day, after psyching myself up for a *really* long time, I went to this gym where I knew they had a daycare. They'd watch your kid while you worked out. And it was so pathetic—I'd go on the treadmill for ten minutes and then I'd jump off and run back to the daycare to check on Olivia. Then back on the treadmill. Then back to the daycare. I think I burned more calories going back and forth to the daycare. But I couldn't fight it. There was something inside me that just did not want me to be away from my daughter.

N: It took me, like, multiple attempts to leave Taylor for the first time. I kept aborting the mission. Mark and I would make plans to go out—but then at the very last moment I couldn't imagine leaving our amazing baby with anyone else. How could another person possibly understand what *my* child wants? Only I can do that! Mark was not impressed. I mean, he was in the car and I was waving to him from the window going, "Sorry, babe, the date's off!"

C: And the lists! I was a huge list leaver. So many details for so many possible outcomes. Every part of the evening routine timed down to the minute. I'm talking military precision, people! One time when Max was little, I went to Bermuda for three days. My mom came to watch the kids. And I was so anal that I left outfits for Max in separate bags for each day that I was away. And each bag had backup diapers in it, and a timed list of how he should spend every single moment without me. Can you imagine how much restraint it took for my mom not to laugh out loud when she saw this?

N: Your mom still talks about it. You also left a bunch of food in the fridge in containers—with the days and times labeled on them. It's like you thought your mom was some alien who had no concept of how to raise a human child.

C: It seemed to make sense at the time. I thought I was just being responsible. Now I go away and sometimes I don't even go grocery shopping before I leave. I'm just, like, "They'll handle it. Someone will handle it."

N: Eventually I did actually go out to dinner with Mark. I didn't leave him sitting in the car forever. It was about five months after Taylor was born, so basically it felt as though I was being released from prison or something. We were both *so* looking forward to it. But I'm pretty sure I ended up being the worst date in the history of couples. I spent the first half of the dinner texting my mom every three minutes, asking, "Is she down yet? Is she crying? Does she miss me?" And then I spent the second part of dinner staring at my phone, looking at the video feed from the camera in her bedroom.

C: Those things are the best and the worst! They give you comfort that your kid is doing okay without you. You can actually see the kid sleeping, so that's good. But they turn you into a crazy person who doesn't pay attention to where she is or what she's doing. You're just staring down the whole time, analyzing every little motion or fidget your baby makes. "Is she waking up? Is she having a bad dream? *We should go home now just in case!*"

N: I've been to parties where I've actually heard moms freaking out, going, "Oh my God, our baby's moving. He's waking up!" Which is such a silly thing to stress about, right? Except I was *exactly* like that a few years ago. They're on their own journey and you've just got to respect that. Part of it is the amazing connection we feel to these little people who grew inside of us for nine months. And part of it is just plain, old-fashioned guilt. Since forever, moms have been conditioned to apologize when we leave our kids to spend our time and our money on our own wants and needs.

C: **The biggest thing for me was realizing that I was thinking about it all wrong. I kept thinking, "I need to be there for them. That's my job. They need me." But then I started seeing it a different way—like, if I go out for a little bit, or I go away for a couple of days, that's a chance for my kids to learn how to take care of themselves. When I take time to work, or work out, or have lunch without kids, or do anything devoted to entirely me, it's okay. Actually, it's better than okay. It shows my family that I matter, too!**

N: Yeah, here are two things we know for sure. First thing: Leaving your kids to do something for yourself can be hard. It's normal to feel selfish. It's programmed into us. But here's the second thing: It's totally worth it. We all need time away, whether it's an afternoon alone or a girls' night out. It just recharges you in a way that nothing else can.

C: **Or imagine this: A whole long weekend away with just your husband. Or the two of you with another couple.**

N: Like, do you have another couple in mind? Mark and I are free.

C: Every part of a trip like that is awesome, beginning at the airport when you show up and realize how much easier it is to travel without kids. No huge diaper bags. No car seats or strollers. No eight pounds of snacks. You wish the flight would never end!

N: Oh my God! Imagine *waking up* when you want to wake up— with only your husband in bed with you, and not somewhere between two and four children. A breakfast all to yourself, and it's not just the crusts from your kids' toast. A whole day spent doing what *you* want to do, with your husband and your best friend and her husband, with no little people yanking on your arm or whining in your ear. Cat, seriously, can we get this going? Bahamas?

C: Imagine an adult conversation that lasts longer than four seconds, over meals that you actually eat while they're warm, while having cocktail after cocktail after cocktail with the fun new friends you met on the flight. New friends who don't have kids, maybe, and won't accidentally remind you of what you've left behind . . .

N: Exactly what are you trying to tell me, Cat?

C: Um, I was hoping you'd watch my kids.

SEVENTEEN

As If We Don't Have Enough to Do, There's Somehow More to Do

Nat

One summer day outside a mall in downtown Toronto, I saw a woman pushing a double stroller along the sidewalk. She looked like a total Badass Mom: walking with purpose, diaper bag tucked underneath, Venti Starbucks coffee in the cupholder, sunglasses on, one earbud in so she could listen to music *and* listen for her children. As she blazed past, I noticed the words on her T-shirt. They were set up to look like an entry in a dictionary. The shirt said, MOTHER: ONE WHO DOES THE WORK OF TWENTY. FOR FREE.

That's not far off! Here's the truth, ladies: When you have a baby, you don't become just a mom. Nope. You instantly inherit a whole bunch of other jobs. Jobs you didn't even apply for. Jobs you probably have zero experience at doing. And guess what? These jobs all start on the same day!

Want to know how clueless Cat and I were? We thought being a mom would be cute. We honestly figured it would be a breeze. We'd love our babies, we'd take care of our babies, we'd hold and feed and change our babies—and then we'd have a long, awesome nap whenever our babies fell asleep. It sounded magical. It sounded *easy*.

Yep, we were dummies. In reality, we barely found a minute for ourselves for years. There are just so many other duties and responsibilities you take on as a mother. Even when you nail the holding and feeding and changing parts of having a baby, there are a bazillion other things you need to do—and other roles you need to play.

Here are just ten of the additional jobs you take on when you become a mom:

1. *Laundry Lady.* When it was just you and your husband, a load of laundry would take, what, maybe five minutes to fold? Tops.

But fill up the washer and dryer with a basket of baby clothes and you're down there for an afternoon! At least it feels that way. Their clothes are so small that you can fit about a hundred onesies and a thousand socks into the same load, and they've all got to be folded or paired. It got so bad that I would literally have nightmares about baby socks. Like, I'd open the dryer in my dreams and millions of the little suckers would just come pouring out like a tidal wave. (By the way, I used to dream mostly about hot guys. What has motherhood done to me?)

2. *Teacher.* "Mommy, why is the sky blue? Why does the doggy's tongue stick out? Why do I have two feet? Why don't I have three feet? Why are 'feet' called feet? Why aren't 'feet' called foots?" Why? Why? *Why? Why??? Why???????*

3. *Nurse/Doctor.* Hey, someone's got to take on the responsibility of diagnosing coughs and sniffles, administering medicine, tending to cuts and scrapes, checking temperatures, and comparing that gross rash to other gross rashes on the Internet.

4. *Maid.* As your child learns to crawl, and then to walk, you begin to notice subtle changes around the house. All of a sudden you can't walk from the living room to the kitchen without stepping on four different stuffed animals and the Weebles musical treehouse. It seems almost scientifically impossible that something so small (a human child) can create a mess so large. But somehow they get the job done. I strongly believe that the back pain I'm going to experience in my fifties will have been caused by years of bending over to pick up pieces of Duplo.

5. *Butler.* "May I pour your bath, Your Majesty? May I fetch you a clean towel, Your Highness? May I have the pleasure of wiping your bum hole after your nightly poop, Your Excellency?"

6. *Actor.* If you don't have kids yet, you're going to think less of me when I say this, but . . . not everything a kid does is interesting. Sorry, but it's true. Sometimes you have to fake it. "Oh, look, what have you drawn for me? *Another* flower? That's twenty-seven straight flowers you've drawn for me. *How interesting!*" With all due respect to Meryl Streep, the best actor in the world is any mom who reacts enthusiastically to the twenty-seventh straight picture of the same flower.

7. *Event Planner.* Four kids means four birthday parties. Which means four *ideas* for birthday parties—ideas that are different from last year's ideas; ideas that are at least as good as the ideas that other moms have had. Yeah, that alone is pretty much a full-time job.

8. *Chef.* I love cooking and I'm pretty great at it, so this one is in my wheelhouse. It's always a pleasure—except for when a kid pipes up with one of her weird food issues. "Mommy, I can't eat my corn now because it touched my potatoes, and I can't eat my ham now because Tucker looked at it funny."

9. *Judge.* Have you ever tried to mediate a dispute between two toddlers? It's like trying to reason with a raccoon. You can talk all you want, but you just know that nothing is ever going to get through. That is why so many moms embrace dictatorship as their preferred form of rule. It's also how the phrase "Because I said so!" was invented.

10. *Chauffeur.* This is a big one as your kids get older and more involved in activities outside the house. I can't even imagine what it's going to be like when we've got four teenagers with four different sets of interests, four different favorite sports, and four different groups of friends. Already, a typical weeknight is like a military operation—with precise pickup and drop-off times around the city. It's like I'm part mom, part Uber.

EIGHTEEN

This Is How to Stop Giving a Shit. Literally.

This is going to be a quick chapter. But it's an important one. To me, it kind of sums up what the first couple years of motherhood are like. I hope that in some weird way it inspires you. But first, it's going to get a little gross. So stick with me!

Our story begins on the morning of a typical winter's day in Toronto—slushy, gray, windy, blah. The kind of day where you just want to curl up and shut out the weather and the world. Except that's not how Cat and Nat roll! Nope. We both just had babies within a few weeks of one another—and we are prepping for our first joint expedition to Starbucks as mothers to five children in total.

The two little ones are already bundled into their Babybjörns. We are mobilizing the three older troops near the front door of my house. Coats, hats, boots, scarves. And then we run through the usual list of questions: Does everyone have their mittens? Has everyone gone to the bathroom? The whole process feels as though it takes slightly less than forever.

We are just about to open the door when Nat says to me, in a casual kind of way, as though friends say this to each other every single day: "Um, Cat, you have either chocolate or shit on your pants."

My first thought: "That's weird. I haven't had any chocolate recently."

Now, some moms—most moms—may have heard Nat's comment and immediately announced: "I need to go change my pants." Chocolate, shit . . . it makes no difference. Time for a clean pair, right?

I reacted a little differently. I found the stain, bent down, and gave it a sniff. I figured: It's got to be chocolate, right? It can't be shit. Turns out I was wrong: It wasn't chocolate. It *was* shit. There was a generous smudge of shit near the knee of my pants.

Here's where we get to the moral of the story. Thank you for bearing with me.

I started trekking upstairs to change—but I stopped halfway. I actually paused there on the step for a few seconds. In the case of the smudge of shit, there was a long list of potential suspects. I had a dog. I had a baby. I had another kid who wasn't toilet trained. But none of that really mattered. The shit was there. The shit was real.

I paused for a second longer. And then I made a decision. I turned around and climbed back down toward the door.

"What are you doing?" Nat asked.

"Let's go," I said. "We're rolling with it."

The kids were ready to go. One of them was strapped to me. Changing my pants would be, at minimum, a ten-minute ordeal— and it could easily set off a chain reaction of crying and bellyaching. No, thank you. We are ready to go to Starbucks and we are going to Starbucks. I am going to Starbucks with shit on my pants.

For a long while, that became my motherhood motto. "I am going to Starbucks with shit on my pants." What it meant was basically: Being a mom is hard, and exhausting, and sometimes literally your greatest accomplishment in a day will be getting through that day.

Sometimes, you just have to persevere. Sometimes, you just have to power through. You can't be concerned with yourself. Sometimes, you just have to go to Starbucks with shit on your pants.

NINETEEN

Toddlers Are Basically Just Small Drunk People

CAT

If you're about to have your baby—or your little one is still an infant—you've probably got a million questions about what lies ahead. How will it feel to be a mother to a toddler? What will the experience be like? Luckily, there is a simple and effective way to prepare—an easy way to get the best possible sense of what the future has in store for you as a mom.

Go hang out with wasted people.

Seriously, you won't believe how much these two groups have in common. How are drunk people and toddlers the same? Here are just ten ways:

1. They feel the need to be physically touching you at all times.

2. They have no filter to stop them from saying inappropriate or offensive things.

3. They may barf on you at any second.

4. They won't regret having barfed on you. In fact, they may not even notice.

5. They feel compelled to be close talkers and loud talkers, even when you can hear them perfectly fine. And even when you tell them to quiet down.

6. As soon as you answer one question, they ask another one.

7. Then they ask that same question again. And again. And over and over and over.

8. They never want to go to sleep.

9. They will scream at you if you try to stop their fun.

10. Even though they are a real handful and they drive you a little bit crazy, they show you so much love that you just can't help but love them right back. Until they barf on you again. That one's a deal breaker.

TWENTY

Let's Get the Heck Off the Hamster Wheel of Guilty Feelings

I *t's 6:30 in the morning.*

The sun is up, the kids are (miraculously) still asleep, and I have the best of intentions. I am totally psyched for this: Today is going to be a great day. Actually, today is going to be the *perfect* day.

Today, I am going to be completely present as a mother. I am going to put my phone away and not look at it even once when I'm around the kids. I am going to be patient and enjoy every single minute with my precious children.

For breakfast, I am going to make them organic fruit smoothies with flaxseed—so they grow up healthy. I am going to shower them with affection. I am going to give each kid some one-on-one time with Mom, so they know they're special. This is the day I nail it as a mother. This is going to be the perfect day.

It is 9:30 in the morning.

Upstairs, I can hear the sound of water pouring onto the bathroom floor from the clogged toilet that the six-year-old keeps flushing. Downstairs, another kid is now ten minutes into ignoring my instructions to get ready to go for a walk. I try to keep it together. Honestly, I try. But I lose it.

"Get your freaking shoes on!"

The kid starts crying. And just like that, I am back on the hamster wheel of guilty feelings.

This goes on in every mom's head.

I shouldn't yell. I know I shouldn't yell.

But sometimes I lose my patience and I yell. Then I feel guilty about it.

I shouldn't let them have a snack right after they have a meal. But sometimes letting them have a treat is just easier than listening to them beg for half an hour. Then I feel guilty about it.

I shouldn't give them mac and cheese again for lunch. They had it yesterday—and the day before. But sometimes I don't have time to go grocery shopping. Then I feel . . . well, you get the idea.

It is 1:30 in the afternoon.

Okay, time to reboot this crazy day.

This is going to be the perfect afternoon. No screen time! In fact, we should really think about canceling cable. Yep, I'm totally going to do it—I'm going to cancel cable. We don't need it! I can help the kids find more productive things to do. I can look on Pinterest and find some nice, calming crafts. I can look on YouTube and teach them to braid each other's hair. We can build a birdhouse together. A birdhouse! Their dad will be so damn impressed.

It is 2:30 in the afternoon.

The kids are watching TV. I know I shouldn't let them. But maybe just for twenty minutes while I return a couple of emails. Wait, it's already been twenty minutes? Okay, then, maybe just one more show.

This is terrible. I'm a terrible mother. They should be playing outside. I should have set up stations outside and they should be moving from one to the next, having a great old time with all my fun, old-fashioned activities.

The hamster wheel of guilt is spinning like crazy.

It is 4:30 in the afternoon.

The kids are quiet in their playroom. Deep down, I know they're probably watching something on the iPad. But if I don't look then I won't know for sure—and I can't feel guilty about it.

I am going to make a great, healthy dinner. I am going to read as many books as they want before bed—and I'm going to read every word. I'm not going to skip words or turn two pages at the same time so I get to the end quicker. I am going to lie there and just chat and snuggle, and I'm not going to rush. It's going to be just like in the movies where the kids are precocious and adorable and the mom is wise and loving and gets foot rubs from Jude Law.

This is going to be the perfect evening.

It is 9:30 at night.

The kids are still awake—and hyper as hell. The dishes are still in the sink. The laundry should be folded in the basket by now, but actually it's still in the washing machine. Did I even start the washing machine? I can't remember. I got distracted when Max dropped a pint of blueberries—then stepped on half of them while coming to tell me that he dropped a pint of blueberries.

Speaking of fruit, I should cut up some strawberries for tomorrow's breakfast. I should make tomorrow's lunches tonight. I bet other moms are making tomorrow's lunches. Better moms than me.

The hamster wheel spins and spins. *Vrrrrrooom!*

I should start a gratitude journal, so I can express how thankful I am. Because I am thankful. Of course I am. Although right now I'd probably just open the journal and write horrible things about blueberries.

I should have sex with my husband, because that keeps the relationship strong. There are a lot of things I should be doing. The Better Moms are probably doing them. The Better Moms write sweet little notes in their kids' school lunches. They lay out their kids' outfits the night before. They stay up late Sunday night making meals for the week to come so they don't get to Wednesday and have to call Domino's like some people (spoiler alert: me). The Better Moms make the beds every single day—not just when they know friends are coming over.

Tomorrow will be different, right? Tomorrow, I will be a Better Mom. Tomorrow, I will get off the hamster wheel of guilty feelings. Tomorrow is going to be a perfect day.

*

Nat and I have been lucky to meet a lot of moms—in the school yard, at conferences, in grocery stores, or through Facebook and Instagram. They've all spent time on the hamster wheel. *Every* mom beats herself up sometimes. They worry that they're being bad moms. That they're too strict or too lenient. Too attentive or too distant. We all feel guilty about something. Sometimes we feel guilty about everything.

But you know what?

We haven't met a mom who isn't trying her hardest. We haven't met a mom who doesn't want the best for her children. We haven't met a mom who doesn't wish for the chance to do better when she's made a mistake.

Each and every day, moms face an insane balancing act. Each and every day, we are responsible for meeting the needs of our kids, while also trying to navigate our own lives.

Each and every day, we make parenting decisions that we *hope* are right. Because let's be honest: No one *really* knows what's right and what's wrong. It's all a big, giant guess—and we can only hope that we make the right choice.

It is so much work to be a mom. It takes so much patience. A mom must tend not only to the immediate needs of her children (feeding them, dressing them, dressing them again when they spill food on their first outfit) but also to the bigger picture. We help them learn confidence, diplomacy, empathy, manners (good luck on that one!), relationships, sensitivity, ambition.

And somewhere in there, we're all supposed to remember that, oh yeah, we're also women—and we need to get our own shit together, clean up the house, and maybe even look banging every now and then.

It's impossible to do all of this—and do it perfectly—every time.

So let's be nicer to ourselves. Let's go easier on ourselves when we screw up. Let's dig deep, stop the hamster wheel of guilty feelings, and climb the heck off—once and for all!

TWENTY-ONE

Tantrums Can Break Your Heart, but Don't Let Them Break Your Spirit

We can sense the Child's tantrum brewing. It is a force of nature, like an approaching tornado—dark and dangerous. We feel the air pressure change. We watch the light fade and the clouds roll in. We see it in the Child's eyes: The storm is coming. As with a tornado, we are powerless to stop it. The Child is powerless to stop it. All that energy has to go somewhere—and we are standing at ground zero. Our only option is to ride it out. Seek shelter and hope for the best.

Then it hits. It is a full-body experience. The toes curl. The eyes bulge. The fists clench. In a flash, the Child is on the floor screaming and shrieking and shouting the absolute worst possible things a little person can think to say. *"I hate you! I've always hated you! You're a terrible mother!"* Anger, fire, venom. *"I wish you were dead!!!!"* Sometimes the Child will slap me for good measure. Other times, there will be scratching or hair pulling—my hair, sometimes; other times, the Child's own hair. More than once, the tantrum has been so intense that the Child has vomited. That was scary. I don't think I've ever felt so lost or powerless, or had my heart ache so much for another human. Nothing I said or did could calm that rage.

We could never predict what would set off the Child. We could never figure out how to stop it. At their worst, these tantrums were happening every couple of days. They sent me seeking the advice of doctors. They ruined more than one family vacation.

I remember one moment in vivid detail, because it was so awful. We were in a souvenir shop in a small town along Cape Cod. My in-laws were there—it was a big family thing. The Child lost it. The Child thrashed on the floor of the shop. The Child sprinted outside and literally walked down the middle of the street, bawling and screeching as *hundreds* of people stopped and looked. They stared at the Child. And, of course, they stared at the loser of a mother who was trailing behind. I'm sure many of them thought the worst of me.

But by then, I had developed a coping mechanism of my own. I knew there was no point in trying to reason with the Child, or comfort, or scold. There was no point in doing anything, other than wait for the storm to pass. On the inside, I was worried. I was furious and frustrated. My heart broke every time, every tantrum. But I trained myself to be like a soldier—to kind of turn myself off and remain stone-faced until the crisis was over. I would just keep thinking, "It will end. This will end. Until then, there's nothing you can do except keep your kid safe."

Not all tantrums are this intense, of course. Let's be honest about it: Some of them can actually be pretty funny to watch.

I remember one trip to the toy store in particular. I know, I know: four kids in a toy store? Rookie mistake, I had it coming. Like letting four foxes into a henhouse and saying, "You can only look." But here's the thing: I usually manage to pull it off. I can almost always get the whole bunch of them in and out with only some mild whining and a few quiet pleas of "Can I have that?" My proven strategy is to make a few vague promises—"Maybe next time, sweetie"—and hustle our asses out of there.

On one particular morning, I was on Item 16 of my endless to-do list: buying gifts for two upcoming birthday parties. I came up with my game plan. I told the kids we were on a mission. I told them we were trying to set a speed record. Back to the car in five minutes. Ready? Go!

I rushed them along the aisles so their eyes couldn't lock on any gadget or gizmo. I distracted them with questions. It was working like a charm. Remember the henhouse? Well, I was counting my chickens before they hatched. I had one gift in hand and the other in sight when it happened—the six-year-old spotted the action figure of his dreams. The one he's seen advertised every single morning on his favorite TV show. I saw him see it—and I knew I was cooked.

"Mommy . . ."

Part of me wanted to get it for him. He wanted it so bad. But if I bought something for one kid, then I would have had to buy something for everyone. Which meant the other three would have had to roam the store until each of them settled on a toy he or she *really* wanted. From past experience, I estimated that this would take roughly nine hours.

"Mommy, I want this . . ."

I tried to distract him.

"Mommy, can I *pleeeeeeeeeeese* . . ."

I was left with no choice. I didn't want to say it. I knew what would happen when I did say it. But I said it.

"No."

In an instant, a kind, soft-spoken boy was transformed into the Loudest Creature on Earth. He raged at top volume. His face turned bright red. *"I want that toy!"*

I grabbed his hand and tried to move on. He ripped his hand away. He dropped to the ground and started flailing. He was on the floor of the Toys "R" Us. He was slapping the floor of the Toys "R" Us. Take that, floor! *I want that toy!* By this point, even my other kids were staring at him and basically going, "Dude, we get what you're trying to do—but take it down a notch."

When you find yourself in this situation (and sorry, Mom, you *will* find yourself in this situation), your first thought may be "What are other people going to think? Are they going to think I'm a terrible mother?" Don't sweat it. Honestly. I remember catching the eye of another mom who was in the same aisle that day in the Toys "R" Us. She just smiled and shrugged. She said a lot with those two small gestures. She said, "Hey, it happens to us all."

It's true. Tantrums happen. Short and intense and often hilarious. And let's face it: They usually happen because you're trying to be a good and responsible mother. So generally speaking, my strategy now is to relax and enjoy the show. The over-the-top screaming. The little limbs flying in all directions. And the insults! They're trying so hard to think of the meanest things they can say to you! So long as they're not physically hurting themselves, they're not hurting anyone. Just let it play out. When they're teenagers, our kids will probably sulk and brood instead. We'll laugh as we think back on all the drama. Sometimes I smile and make mental notes. When they grow up, I want to be able to remind them of what they used to call me. *Oh, so you want to borrow the car, do you? Then maybe you shouldn't have called me a BIG, DUMB DUMMY twelve years ago.*

But the more intense tantrums—like the Child's tantrums—can be frightening. They can be physically draining for kid and parent alike. The most heartbreaking thing is that once the switch flips, the Child has little if any control over what is happening. These words and actions are not a conscious choice. They are biology. They are an eruption. Over time, we have developed a routine where I simply say, "Let me know when you're done." And five minutes later, or ten, or sometimes forty-five, the storm subsides and the Child crawls into my lap. There is instant remorse. Sometimes, the Child looks up at me and says, "I didn't catch myself in time." That's a lot for a kid to have to deal with.

But there is something else you should know about the Child: The same heat that fuels the tantrums also powers a loving and passionate heart. The Child cares more than most, and feels more than most, and is willing to give more than most. There is a greater intensity. There is a deeper affection. The Child falls harder but soars higher.

These days, the Child's tantrums are fewer and they are less intense. There is a greater ability to control the storm within—to channel that energy differently. There was no magic moment when things began to change. It happened slowly and naturally as the Child grew older.

The name of the Child does not matter. This is my child. It could be your child. It could be your nephew or niece, or the son of a friend, or a girl you see one day on the street. You are not a bad mom if your kid has a tantrum. Your son or daughter isn't crazy or disturbed. Children need to learn how to express themselves. Each of them learns differently. They need to understand the emotions within before they can begin to try to control them. Each of them understands at a different pace.

You are there to help them as best you can. Sometimes, helping them means nothing more than keeping them safe as you wait for the storm to pass, the clouds to part, and the blue sky to return.

THEY NEVER WARN YOU ABOUT THE STUPID FRIGGIN' BEES!

C: Ready for a scorching hot take from Cat and Nat? Like, multiple flame emoji hot? 🔥🔥🔥

N: Brace yourself! Here it comes: We hate the park.

C: Hate it.

N: Moms aren't supposed to hate the park. We're supposed to love it. We're supposed to spend hours there during long summer days, lazing on a blanket while our children learn valuable social skills and engage in a voyage of creative and physical discovery on the play structure. It's supposed to be a magical, wonderful place where we can find an oasis of peace in our hectic lives and bluebirds land on our shoulders and sing softly in our ears.

C: That's all bullshit. The park is dirty and gross.

N: *So* gross.

C: Can you imagine the stuff that has been dropped, spilled, thrown, peed, and barfed onto that play structure? It makes a carnival ride or the bathroom floor at a rock concert seem hygienic. And by the way, who uses the park after the sun goes down? Teenagers and homeless people. Think about that. Your kid is playing in a homeless man's living room. And just think of all the fun they can have with the Bacardi bottles and condom wrappers that the teenagers left behind.

N: But that's just the beginning. The park also attracts tons of random strangers who could totally be there to run off with your child. You don't know! So you're constantly on high alert. You always have to worry about somebody being kidnapped. Which, by the way, is superstressful.

C: Exactly! Which part of this amazing park experience is supposed to be relaxing for the mom? You can't sit down. You can't look away. You've got to track your kid like a hunter following his prey. And guess what, guys? I don't have three eyes. How am I supposed to watch three children with just two eyes?

N: Have you ever actually paid attention to what's happening *on* the play structure? It's not some Pixar movie scenario where all the kids are working hand in hand to achieve perfectly harmonious playtime. It's *Lord of the Flies* up there. It's survival of the fittest. Big kids shoving little kids. Bullies, lunatics, weirdos, psychological warfare. Kids climbing, slipping, stumbling, falling.

C: What is with these play structures anyway? They're huge, and they're usually built to ensure that every ten feet or so there's an awesome place for a kid to fall or bonk himself on the head. Next time you go to the park, start the timer on your phone and see how long it takes before some kid starts bawling. There's like a head injury every three minutes.

N: It's like some engineers got together and said, "Ladies and gentlemen, our mission is to increase the number of childhood concussions. Let's start by putting in at least three very high platforms for no reason. Then we'll add an impossible climbing wall and a fireman's pole, so the weaker children can learn how to plummet really far."

C: And if your kids don't get hurt—and by the way, they *will* get hurt, but if somehow they don't—they'll wind up getting stuck in a tunnel and you won't be able to get them out. Or the slide will be all sticky (probably from some other kid's barf), and it'll take, like, three minutes for the kid to get down it. So much fun! The world's slowest and stickiest barf slide!

> *N:* And you're there trying to convince them that they're having a blast: "Oh, *boy*! Here we go so fast down the slide! *Wheeeee!*" But they know you're full of shit.

C: By the way, getting them on the nonsliding slide is actually the best-case scenario. Why? Because it never fails: The minute you get to the park, your kid needs to either pee or poo. And is there ever a place nearby to pee or poo? Of course not. So it's either back home or into the bushes.

> *N:* But you know what? You don't have to listen to us. You don't have to see it our way. Maybe *you* love the park. Some moms definitely do. Maybe it's your favorite place. Maybe you love how it's muddy in the spring and scalding hot in the summer. Maybe you just can't get enough of the shrieking children and the sand blowing into your eyes.

C: Maybe you just love the never-ending feeling of dread that comes from knowing that, at any given moment, a pedophile could be circling the park in his windowless van. And don't forget the bees. There are always so many wasps and bees. I hate bees even more than I hate the grass. They don't warn you about the bees!

> *N:* There are so many moms at the park, and, sure, most of them are nice—but then you always end up stuck talking to the one crazy mom who won't shut up about vaccines or food preservatives. Listen, I am totally down with some mom chitchat. I'm social and I'm nice—up to a point. But the problem is that the park is a stationary, contained environment.

C: You see someone at the grocery store—you stop and say hi, you chat for two minutes, you move on to the produce section. Done. But the only polite way to crowbar yourself out of a conversation at the park is to leave the park. You can't just say, "Look, it's been great standing here for forty-five minutes as you describe your son's legendary clarinet skills to me, but now I'm going to move slightly over there so I can get away from you and your crazy mouth."

> *N:* That totally reminds me: another reason we hate the park? Competitive snack displays.

C: Some moms roll into the park with picnic baskets the size of steamer trunks. And they'll be laying out all these perfect little Tupperware containers filled with perfectly chopped vegetables and perfectly cut-up pieces of fruit and dainty little gluten-free sugar-free cookies. These moms are awesome and I totally want to punch them.

> *N:* Because our kids see this feast and they're, like, "Where are *our* snacks?" And then I have to be the mom who scrounges

around in her purse and goes, "Uh, I think I have one Mentos left. You guys can split it four ways."

C: By the way, who has the time to put together these gourmet snack buffets? Did you get up at 3:00 a.m.? Are you a vampire mom? I didn't even have time to change out of the yoga pants that I stained before I left the house, but now I'm pretending I just stained them here at the park.

N: You know what else I hate about the park? Swings. Sorry, kids, this is going to blow your minds, but Mommy doesn't want to push you for two hours. It's boring. It's the most boring thing in the world.

C: Also, last time I checked, parks don't serve wine.

N: Yeah, that's a deal breaker.

C: What do you hate more? The park—or playdates?

 N: Whoa, that's actually a tough one. As much as I hate play structures and grass and bees, I think it might actually be playdates. Because here's the truth about being a mom, okay? You love your own kids, obviously. And you like a lot of other kids. But you don't like *every* kid.

C: I mean, you don't show it! You don't, like, give a toddler the finger or anything.

N: But some kids are annoying. Or weird. Or violent or filthy or, like, crazy unpredictable. Or they're always mean to your kid.

Or they're sick all the time and they bring their runny noses and their gross coughs into your house, and you just know that five days later *everyone* is going to have that cold. It's, like, come on, other moms—keep those snot factories at home.

C: I'm just going to come out and say it: I don't like wiping other kids' asses. I can barely muster the willpower to do it for my own kids. I understand the biology of it. I understand that it's not their fault— they're little and they need help. I understand that, at the end of the day, there's really not much difference between my son's ass and some other kid's ass. But still, come on, no thanks.

N: Let's not forget the drop-off conversations.

C: The worst! Okay, Moms, here's the etiquette—and please pay attention, because some people just can't seem to grasp this.

N: I don't need to talk to you for twenty minutes when you drop off your kid, and another twenty when you pick him up. I've got shit to do. Let's keep it to a tight three minutes at drop-off and ninety seconds at pickup. Get in, get out, get on with our lives.

C: And if you desperately need a comprehensive debrief of how the afternoon went, then you need to attach a GoPro to your kid's head and run through the footage when you get home. I am not a stenographer, and the truth is I only barely paid attention.

N: We need to come up with a contract for potential playdates. We need parents to certify that their kids are independent,

potty-trained, polite, and healthy—and then, sure, come on over!

C: Or you know what? You can take our kids anytime. Anytime at all. We're happy to drop all seven of them off. Maybe you could take them to the park. We hear that going to the park is awesome.

N: **Just watch out for the bees.**

TWENTY-THREE

Let's Raise Our Kids to Be Honest . . . by Lying to Them!

Sunday morning at 7:45, and there is peace in our home. The children—all four of them!—are playing quietly. My husband is still asleep. And I'm sitting on the couch drinking a coffee and thinking the one thought that has preoccupied mothers for hundreds of years: How much longer can this last before it turns back into the usual gong show?

The answer: About twelve minutes. And believe me: When the morning calm falls apart, it falls apart in a hurry.

A scream of pain. A shriek of innocence. Accusations. Denials. Claims of someone punching someone else. And some of the more creative name-calling you're ever going to hear. (I believe it was my daughter, a few years back, who invented the term "Dumbstupidface.")

What's a mother to do? I go all *Law & Order* on the situation. I interview the witnesses to the alleged physical assault. And when I'm confident that the prime suspect is in fact guilty of the allegation, I bring out the most powerful weapon known to either mother or father: the Lie.

"Teddy," I say softly, "am I going to have to call him?"

Teddy knows who "him" is.

"No," Teddy says. "Please don't call him."

I raise my cell phone and start dialing. Well, I *pretend* to start dialing, but Teddy doesn't know that. Poor, trusting Teddy.

"No! Don't!" he yells and tries to grab my phone.

"I sure hope he doesn't take you away," I say, as though I'm actually worried.

"No, please don't call him! It's okay! I hit Tucker and I'm sorry! *I'm really sorry!*"

This, fellow moms, is a little ploy that I like to call the Fake

Phone Call to a Fake Authority Figure. I highly recommend it because it can be adapted to almost any scenario. Just grab your phone, peck at the screen, and then put the phone to your ear. "Hello, Officer—I have a son here who needs to be picked up and taken away. He's been bad and he needs to go to bad-boy jail." You'd be surprised how effective this is. Fear of the unknown, I guess. I'd love to be able to look into my son's brain and see how he pictures "bad-boy jail."

I'm sure that, by now, you're starting to understand that we are *so* not the "perfect moms." We try like heck. We do our best. But you're never going to look at us and go, "Now there's a pair of mothers who've got it down to a science."

Case in point: We are certainly not above lying to our children to make our lives a little easier. Sounds horrible, I know. But we don't really think of them as "lies." We think of them as examples of "Mommy using her imagination." It's all about getting our kids to do what we want or need them to do. Here are just a few more of the lies we tell our kids the most:

"Santa is watching." This is a supereffective and time-tested way to get a child to alter his behavior, at least for a little while. It's been in use for generations! Rookie moms play this card in December—but pros like us have figured out how to use it year-round. "Hey, TJ, stop stealing your sister's sand pail. Santa is watching. Yep, he's renting a cottage on the same lake as us. So smarten up or else."

"Every photo you take goes to the cloud, where mommies and daddies can see them." This is more of a preemptive lie. We're trying

to lay the groundwork to ensure that no one is eventually tempted to use an electronic device to take any sort of "naughty" pic. Most adults can't quite figure out what the friggin' cloud is, so you can imagine how it would confuse a nine-year-old.

"If you don't eat your fruits and vegetables, you will be weak forever." I'll admit it: This one isn't particularly creative or clever. Then again, it may not even be a lie! It fits into the same genre of part lie, part exaggeration as "If you don't get a haircut, you're going to get lice" (I use that one) and "If you don't brush your teeth, they will turn brown and fall out."

"If I have to tell you one more time . . ." This might be one of the all-time most-used lies in the history of motherhood. *If I have to tell you one more time to get dressed, we're not going to the hockey game!* Truth is, of course, we paid a small fortune for the tickets, so we are definitely going. Eventually, one of my kids is going to figure out that I'm completely full of shit with threats like these. Then I'll either need to knock it off with the fibs—or maybe (probably) just come up with a more convincing lie!

"If you don't do your homework, you're going to be homeless." This one is going to stop being useful the moment one of our kids discovers that neither Cat nor I exactly killed it in high school. (We both ended up getting our diplomas by going to night school!)

"The zoo is closed on long weekends because the animals go away." This is one of my all-time best lies, if I do say so myself. I spent the

entire week bribing my kids. I told them that if they were good, we'd go to the zoo on the weekend as a family. It worked like a charm. All four of them were angels. But when the weekend arrived, I saw a bunch of posts online saying the zoo was so packed that it was, well . . . a zoo. So I pulled this excuse out of my ass. Not only did it work, but the kids also spent an hour discussing where tigers would go on their "vacation." It may not have been the truth, but it got the job done.

And that's the point, really. We'd never lie to our kids about anything that's really important—or anything that would cause them to stress out. We just do it to gently guide them toward more mature behavior. And also sometimes we do it because it's fun. They're so easy to trick!

Let's just hope we don't get taken away to bad-mom jail!

TWENTY-FOUR

Your Kids Will Be Who They Are, Not Who You May Expect Them to Be

When your child is in kindergarten, parent-teacher night is usually a pretty low-stress affair. I mean, what is there really to talk about with the teacher? Has my kid mastered the complex art of finger painting? Does he or she almost always remember to return from the bathroom wearing pants? The bar for nailing it in kindergarten is not superhigh.

But when our daughter Olivia was in kindergarten, her teacher greeted us with a handshake and a look of concern. Marc and I knew what was coming. We'd been worried about it, too. "You have such a lovely daughter," the teacher began, working up to the ". . . but."

"But she's so shy."

We nodded our heads. This wasn't exactly breaking news to us. Our firstborn had always been quiet and introverted in any kind of social situation. We're not talking about the regular kind of shyness, where it takes a kid a little while to warm up to a new person or environment. That's pretty common. Olivia was in a whole different league. She was an all-star at being silent and withdrawn.

Olivia's teacher was polite and supportive. But he was also frank. "I honestly don't know if Olivia knows my name, or if she knows the alphabet. I've spent a year and a half with her now, and I don't think I've ever heard her speak."

Few people had. Olivia wouldn't go on playdates. She wouldn't go to birthday parties. She wouldn't talk to her classmates. As a little girl, Olivia loved to dance—but we couldn't get her to take a dance class. At home, she would talk freely with us. But she wouldn't do anything that involved any human other than her mommy and her daddy.

It was hard to see her like this. But it was even harder to see the effect on her. Olivia's life was a never-ending roller coaster of relief and anxiety. She'd come home happy that school was over. But by bedtime, she'd be getting worked up about having to go back in the morning. It would eat at her. "My stomach hurts," she'd tell us. "My stomach hurts so much." If ever there was a substitute teacher, Olivia would simply refuse to go to class. Spend the school day with a total stranger? Not a chance. She didn't talk to her regular teacher, but I guess she at least felt comfortable around him.

I think every mom has that moment when she thinks to herself: Is my kid always going to be like this? Is he always going to insist on wearing soft pants instead of jeans? Is he always going to take off his shirt in the grocery store? Is she always going to walk into a social situation and literally crawl under a table?

When I was a little girl, I was independent and outgoing. Think of a precocious sitcom character with pigtails and a sassy attitude— that was me. I'd strike up conversations with strangers in the grocery store or at the park. I'd tell them my name and ask them questions about their lives. I'd tell them about my family and our plans for the weekend. I remember one older lady chuckling at my endless chitchat and calling me "a big ball of fire."

I guess I kind of assumed that my daughter would be like me. I mean, I didn't obsess over it or anything. It just seemed logical to me: I was outgoing. She'd be watching me and learning from me, and she also shared my genes. So she'd be outgoing, too.

When it didn't turn out that way, Marc and I were worried, obviously. We didn't know what to do. It's not easy to watch your child struggle. It can be superfrustrating. More than anything, you want to reason with the kid. You want to just tell her: "Look, life is going to be hard for you if you can't learn to talk to other people. So just do it!"

For a long time, Marc and I held on to the hope that something would trigger the end of this phase of Olivia's life—and the beginning of a new period when she would begin to interact with the world around her.

At home, she seemed happy. She'd smile and play. She was thoughtful and generous. But she just shut down the split second that someone else stepped into her world. It was so hard not to freak out. But there was one thing that helped. It turned out that Olivia had a lot in common with . . . Nat! And getting the two of them together made a big difference in Olivia's life.

As a woman, Nat is a big-time extrovert. I have literally seen her dance on a tabletop in public—and not just once. But as a little girl she was crazy shy. She refused to look anyone in the eye. She wouldn't talk to her teachers or classmates. As Nat tells it, she was almost literally attached to her mother. Wouldn't go anywhere without her. Wouldn't talk to anyone who wasn't her. I remember Nat once saying that it caused her physical pain to be put in the position of having to talk to a stranger. "It wasn't charming, it wasn't cute," she said. "People thought there was something wrong with me."

Nat's shyness lasted until the second grade, when she discovered that she was interested in boys—and the only way to get their attention was to, you know, talk to them. She came out of her shell in a hurry. Nat loves to tell the story that, on her eighth birthday, two boys in class each brought a present to school. One gave her a bouquet of baby's breath. The other gave her a dollar bill. "My mom took me to his house and made me give back the dollar, which was so mortifying," she says. "But all the other girls were jealous anyway."

But to our credit, we made an important decision. We decided not to panic. We figured that pressuring Olivia—or forcing her to be someone that she's not—would only send her deeper into her shell. So we lived with Olivia on her terms. Nat helped guide her along, but we didn't push her. We didn't force her into anything. We didn't apologize to people for her refusal to respond to them. Instead, we encouraged her. We gently nudged her. We accepted her decisions. We did things her way—and we waited.

It was hard. But today, at age nine, Olivia is a very different girl. She talks to her teacher. She has two best friends. She actually got up onstage and performed in front of the entire school, which is something we honestly thought would never happen. There was no One Big Miracle like in a made-for-TV movie. It wasn't like a switch flipped. It happened over time—at her pace, when she was ready. It happened with our support, but it happened on her terms.

As a mom, you will never learn more than from your firstborn. That first kid teaches you about yourself, about your strengths and weaknesses, about your limits. She teaches you patience and understanding. She teaches you the best way to teach her.

Your impulse may be to show him everything, map things out for him, give him all the answers. It's a natural instinct: You want to protect her. But it's actually hugely important to let her lead the way sometimes. You have to trust that she'll find her own path, even if it's hard for her and hard for you. You have to walk beside him, not ahead of him.

The kid you see today will be different in a few years. He may be different in a few months. He will grow, and evolve, and learn, and change. He will become a new version of himself, many times over. The girl who speaks with a stutter may conquer it during summer vacation. The boy who one year quakes in fear and cries during the school concert—may turn out to be the lead in next year's school play.

And one shy little girl may step slowly and warily out of her own world and find the courage to say her teacher's name.

TWENTY-FIVE

Welcome to Our Adventures in Bad Mom-ing

Nat

You think you've ever screwed up as a mom? Hold my beer.

It's a beautiful August day in the north of Ontario. Just trees and lakes and rocks and the best sounds and smells you can imagine. My family is there, Cat's family is there—all eleven of us just hanging out on the dock, enjoying a morning coffee. Cat and I are congratulating ourselves for nailing it in the Mom department this week. The kids are having a blast, jumping in the water and splashing around and trying to catch minnows. We're basically spending our vacation inside the perfect Canadian postcard.

My phone rings. I look at the screen: "Mom cell." Hmm, that's weird. It's not like her to call this early when she knows we're away.

"Hey, Mom, what's up?"

"I'm just calling to speak to the birthday boy."

My heart stops. Birthday boy? *Who is the birthday boy?*

I am so shocked, by the way, that I actually say those words out loud. I say them out loud for everyone to hear. *"Who is the birthday boy?"*

There is a pause on the other end of the line. Then, what sounds like a giggle. "Um, today is TJ's second birthday, Natalie."

I gasp. I literally gasp. I don't know what to do. I freeze in place.

Mark starts laughing. Cat starts laughing. Through the phone, I can hear my mom start laughing.

I hang up and pause for a moment. Well, this is a pretty epic Mom fail, isn't it, Nat? *Or is it?* Maybe it's not too late to save the day! Without any plan in mind at all, I leap up from my chair. I grab a towel, wave it in the air, and start shouting, "Listen up, everyone! It's TJ's birthday! Let's all . . . go to the kitchen!"

Why did I wave a towel in the air? I have no idea. Why did I order everyone to go to the kitchen? I have no idea. How long did it take the other kids to figure out that I'd forgotten TJ's birthday and I was desperately trying to cover my ass? Not very long. Kids are actually pretty smart that way.

Unfortunately, the walk from the dock to the kitchen is so short that it doesn't give me enough time to come up with a reason why I am making everyone walk from the dock to the kitchen. We arrive and everyone stares at me. My mouth starts moving, and I begin speaking, which is interesting to me because I have no idea what I am about to say.

"Okay, everyone! Let's gather together. Actually, let's get in a circle. Yeah, a circle! And now everyone . . . Let's sing 'Happy Birthday' to TJ!"

That's it. That's my whole plan. We sing "Happy Birthday." Everyone gives TJ a hug. And then, awkwardly, everyone just kind of wanders back down to the dock. I am left alone with TJ in the kitchen. I know this seems like a kind of abrupt and anticlimactic end to the story, but that's how it happened in real life. There was a brain cramp of epic proportions—an all-out failure of the Mom mind. There was a half-assed attempt to make up for it. And then everyone went on with their day.

But back to me in the kitchen. I suppose I could have cried and beaten myself up over forgetting my baby's birthday. And for a moment, I did curse at myself under my breath. But then I laughed. I mean, he was only two, right? It wasn't like he was even going to remember the Weird Spur-of-the-Moment Kitchen Circle Birthday Song. He wasn't going to remember that his mother completely forgot the anniversary of his birth. He wasn't going to remember any of it . . . until he read this chapter . . . or any of the other six kids mentioned it to him, which they've already done about 437 times since that day. *Remember when your dumb mom totally forgot your birthday, TJ?*

So, yeah, I have my bad days just like anyone else. Same goes for Cat. We've done (more than) our share of stuff that wouldn't exactly put us in contention for a Kick-Ass Mom of the Year award.

But that's part of the journey, right? Not every day can be golden. Sometimes you forget the birthday of the cutest two-year-old boy in the world. Sometimes you say the wrong thing at the wrong time. Sometimes you botch a day so bad that the goal becomes getting to bedtime by any means necessary. In the spirit of coming clean, here are ten other sketchy things that do happen or have happened on our watch:

1. Occasionally we feed the kids noodles twice a day with barely any veggies. Other times we have cake pops and hot chocolate with whipped cream for no reason at all.

2. Four words: Uber Eats for breakfast.

3. Every once in a while, we urge the kids to beg their daddy to take them to the park—but, of course, Mommy has to stay at home because the baby is sleeping.

4. One day when we were together and both of us were at a low point, we put on Netflix and just left it running. All day. The kids thought they were in heaven. They kept looking at us as if to say, "So you guys have finally given up, eh?"

5. Once in a while, we'll say no when one of our kids asks us to play. Horrible, right? Truth is, we both hate playing with our kids. We

just don't have the patience to pretend to be a fairy godmother or a unicorn or whatever. Maybe that's part of the reason our families hang out together every damn day—so our kids have other little people to play with.

6.   We bring electronic devices to restaurant dinners and let the kids play the whole time, just to stop them from whining or from getting up and wandering around the place, touching other people's meals.

7.   One rough Saturday in particular, we cracked open a bottle of tequila. At 1:45 in the afternoon.

8.   Maybe you think you sometimes let your kids watch too much TV. But can you beat our record? One time, our seven kids woke up from a sleepover and watched the movie *Frozen* two times—before 8:30 a.m.!

9.   Okay, we take no pride in saying this, but at least once we have pretended to have diarrhea in order to get a twenty-minute break in the bathroom. (No regrets!)

10. On very rare occasions, we attempt "adulting" with the kids in tow. One time, the two of us loaded up seven kids (plus a niece) and headed for a cool adult restaurant in our neighborhood. One kid took off his shirt. Another spent 80 percent of the dinner under the table. The rest of them went to the bathroom about seven hundred times. But we did it. Obviously, we tried to be respectful of others around us. Well, we *tried* to try. Mostly we had margaritas and didn't stress about the mayhem.

TWENTY-SIX

Up Yours, Honey Nut Cheerios Bee

$\int$hortly before ten o'clock on a Tuesday morning, I reach up into the cupboard and take down one of the small pink plastic bowls. I put it on the counter. Then I step to the right to grab the box of Honey Nut Cheerios.

Suddenly, I freeze. I am overcome by a thought: I've done this before. I've poured Honey Nut Cheerios into this exact bowl at this exact time of day—so the same child can have the same snack. In fact, I've poured Honey Nut Cheerios into this *exact* bowl, at pretty much this *exact* time, for what feels like two hundred days in a row. Or four hundred. Or maybe a million.

I stare at that goddamn Honey Nut Cheerios bee. I see him more than I see my husband. I am overcome with the urge to throw the box at the wall or on the floor. I want to do something different. *Anything* that's different from what I always do.

Have you ever seen the old Bill Murray movie *Groundhog Day?* His character is cursed to live the same day over and over—the same people, the same place, the same routine. Over and over and over until he can predict pretty much every moment of his existence. That's pretty much the life of a mom with young children! It's, like, "Is the toddler having a freak-out and throwing his banana pieces on the floor? It must be 1:07 p.m., because this happens every day at 1:07 p.m."

In some ways, routine can be great. It gives kids the opportunity to develop skills. It teaches them structure. It provides at least some element of predictability to a day. But the routine of motherhood can make it feel as though your entire life is an endless loop of menial tasks. Some days, I savor the familiarity. There's a comfort to putting it on autopilot and just getting to bedtime. But the routine can also grind you down. It can drain you of energy and sap your spirit.

It can leave you deep in a Mom Rut.

Out of the blue, everything about being a mother feels harder than it normally does. The kids fight more. They listen to you less. Time crawls by. Nothing you do seems to make it any easier. Nothing anyone says to you seems to make it any better. Will it ever be wine o'clock?

Welcome to the monotony of motherhood. Welcome to life as that Bill Murray character at his lowest point, when he's convinced his life will *always* be this one same day (except you don't have time to learn French poetry and ice sculpture, so you're actually worse off than he is). Being overwhelmed by the tedium of it all doesn't mean you don't love your kids. It doesn't mean you're down on motherhood. It just means you're human. Like I said to Nat one time, "It's like I don't feel like being a mom today." Which is tough beans, of course, because there's no phoning in sick or skipping out from being a parent. It's a 24/7 job with no vacation time.

For me, the important realization was that Mom Ruts are totally normal. Everyone gets caught up in them from time to time. Here's what Nat and I do to break out of the Mom Rut:

1. *Acknowledge the rut.* It actually helps to say it out loud: "I'm in a rut." You're telling yourself, "I need to do something about this." You become aware that you can change your own situation. This sounds obvious, but it can actually be very helpful. I think we're all kind of programmed by society to expect that motherhood is going to be nonstop bliss. So we feel kind of bad about ourselves for having these feelings of boredom and frustration. But they're normal! It's normal not to love every single phase of your kid's upbringing. And it's normal not to feel bliss when you're making eye contact yet again with that Honey Nut Cheerios bee.

2. *Even small tweaks to your regular schedule can make a big difference.* The easiest thing to do is to default to your usual patterns. It takes effort to change things up. So force yourself to break your own habits. Serve breakfast for dinner as part of Backwards Day. Take the kids to a different park, at a different time of day. Or better yet, carve out a little time for yourself. Get a babysitter or a relative to step in at a time when you would normally *never* be free to do what you want. Go see a matinee. Go have lunch on your own—just you and your phone or a book. Go sit under a tree and fall asleep for twenty minutes. Honestly, even an hour away from your usual routine can feel like an absolute gift, and can send you back home with more energy and a new attitude.

3. *Turn the tables.* Have your kids make lunch for *you*. Have them tell *you* a story at bedtime. You change up the dynamic when you change the rules.

4. *Accept that not every moment has to be a perfect moment.* This is a big one. Everyone with older kids is always warning you, "The time goes by so fast!" They keep telling you, "You've got to soak up every moment!" This is—to be polite—bullshit.

First of all, it would be easier to enjoy every second if the seconds were easier to enjoy. Know what we mean? Do you ever watch sports highlights on TV? They take a three-hour game and they reduce it to just thirty or forty seconds by focusing on only the best and worst parts of the game.

Most of mothering is like the rest of that game. It's days that blend together. It's nighttime rituals that are repeated for months or even years. Some days are "just get through the day" kinds of days, and that's okay.

It's okay to have a bad day and go to bed thinking, "I'm glad that's over." It's okay to have a dull day that will never be remembered in a scrapbook. It doesn't diminish how much you love your kids, or how much you cherish being a mom.

Once you accept that, you begin to climb out of the Mom Rut. You get closer to daylight.

You know how kids go through phases? Moms do, too. If you work at it, the Mom Rut phase will pass. And when it does, you'll be amazed by how much easier everything suddenly seems.

TWENTY-SEVEN

It Can Be Damn Hard to Keep Calm and Carry On

Nat

Welcome to another typical night in the madhouse. Let me give you a tour of our scene of domestic bliss.

In one bedroom, two of our kids are fighting over . . . *something*. I'm too tired to bother getting the details. I just keep hearing one of them yell, "Your stupid butt stinks!" Solid burn, buddy. Meanwhile, down the hall, another child is just randomly shrieking for no apparent reason. It's the kind of piercing sound that travels straight from your ears to your very last nerve. Every mother knows this sound. Every mother hates it. *This* mother really hates it.

When they're babies, this is known as the "witching hour"—that daily period of fussiness that never seems to end. My kids are a little older now, so I call it the "bitching hour." Time for everyone to complain about something: bedtimes, homework, their brother, their sister, their mother. (Usually it's their mother.)

But tonight, our quartet is a trio. One of our kids is unusually quiet. It's Taylor, our oldest. She ran cross-country at school in the afternoon, and I'm worried she may be a bit dehydrated. She's complaining of a headache. As the circus rages around us, I give her a little extra attention, tucking her into bed like she's a little girl again.

To be honest, I'm kind of savoring this—a rare moment when my little Taye doesn't mind being doted on by her mother. Like all wild spirits, Taylor can be a handful. One time, I remember saying to Cat: "I wish I could see her through the eyes of others." Her teachers, her friends, other parents—they look at Taylor and they see an amazing, outgoing little girl. I see that, too. But I also see a different side.

How can I describe it? It's like she's two different people. Out in the world, she's kind and respectful. At home, she can sometimes be stubborn and quick to anger. A totally awesome kid—but one who seems to save all her naughtiness for me. I bet a lot of moms know that feeling.

But there's no fight in Taylor tonight. I lean down, give her a kiss on the forehead, and turn to switch off her bedside light. And that's when I see it. There on the table next to her bed. A bottle of vitamin D pills.

An *empty* bottle of vitamin D pills.

An empty bottle of *150* vitamin D pills that I'd bought less than a week ago.

Uh, Taye . . . *Where did all the pills go?*

Silence. Shifty eyes. That guilty look.

And then, finally: "I ate them."

I can't remember the exact order in which the following thoughts raced through my head, but I think it went like this: My girl is going to die. My girl has poisoned herself. She's going to grow a third arm. She's going to need her stomach pumped. She's going to turn green and acquire superstrength. She's going to have brain damage. She's never going to be the same.

She's *never* going to be the same.

All that took about half a second. There was a jolt of fear, and, believe me, fear is never rational when it's about your kids. The Mom brain is the most efficient machine ever created for coming up with worst-case scenarios.

As a parent, I always struggle with my reaction in a moment of crisis. My natural approach is to explode. It's biological. It's almost as though I can physically feel it rising within me. But nobody wants to be like that. Nobody wants to be the mom in the mall who starts shrieking because her little boy dropped his ice cream cone.

Knowing this is the easy part. Acting on it, for me at least, is harder. In between bursts of profanity, I did some quick math using the back of the vitamin D bottle. The recommended daily dose (and the contents of one pill) is 400 IU. That means Taylor took . . . 60,000 IU. So, yeah, I think I'll take this moment to *freak the hell out*. I mean, I know vitamins aren't toxic. But isn't pretty much *everything* toxic when you take 150 times the recommended dose?

I took out my phone even before I'd decided whom to call. I paused for a moment and thought it through. If I called my mom, I know exactly what she'd say. She'd say, "Don't worry about it, everything's going to be fine." My mom has been saying that for forty years. It's her guiding philosophy. On her tombstone, it's going to say: DON'T WORRY ABOUT IT, IT'LL BE FINE.

Instead, I phoned the number for the local poison control hotline. I had to be sure—and I wasn't going to trust some rando's blog on the Internet. As I dialed, I decided that I was going to make this one of those "teachable moments" the experts are always talking about. I got Taylor out of bed and made her listen to the call. I was probably a little too intense and a little too angry. I could see that Taylor was scared. The woman on the other end of the phone caught wind of what I was trying to do. She explained that Taylor was in no danger, but she also emphasized the risk of taking pills of any kind—even colorful, cartoony ones—without parental supervision. Taylor kept holding my hand. She was worried because I seemed worried.

I wanted to make sure all the kids got the message. And so early the next morning, I put on my Bad Cop hat and started the interrogation. The story began to come together. Taylor hadn't eaten *all* the vitamins. She'd distributed some of them to her siblings and to Cat's

kids. Turns out everyone wanted a few because the vitamins were fla-
vored to taste basically like candy. The good news: Taye was exposed
to fewer IUs than I'd originally feared. The bad news: Not only was
our daughter a pill popper—but she was also a pusher. Do you think
all great entrepreneurs get started this way?

The thing about being a mom is that you become hypervigilant.
You see danger in everything. Those scissors. That knife. That Halloween candy. But kids are pretty clever. They find trouble in ways
you can never predict. You can do your best. You can watch them
damn near close to 24/7. And they'll still find ways to surprise you.

And it's hard to know how to react. You don't want to be the
mom who goes bananas every time her kids get within ten feet of a
safety pin. You want them to learn to figure stuff out on their own
and walk it off when they get hurt. But there's always the risk that . . .
Well, let me tell you a story.

When I was a little girl, I fell at school and landed on my shoulder. It hurt like hell. When I got home, my mom (her name is Gisele)
gave it a quick squeeze and said, "It'll be fine." (See? I told you. It's
her guiding philosophy.) I trusted that she was right. I was a little
kid—it had never occurred to me that mothers could be wrong. But
the pain didn't go away. In fact, it kept getting worse. I couldn't con-
centrate in school. "It'll be fine," my mom said. I couldn't sleep. I felt
sick to my stomach.

Finally, after a few days, my mom gave in and took me to the
doctor. Verdict: broken collarbone. Did my mom apologize to me?
She did not. The doctor gave me a sling to wear and some pills for
the pain. As we got into the car, my mom patted me on the thigh and
said just one thing: "You'll be fine."

How would you have reacted in this situation? Would you have been pissed off at your mom for not taking you to the doctor right away? I wasn't. Yes, my mom was definitely a bit too chill this one time. But, even at a young age, I appreciated how natural and confident she was at being a mother. She never second-guessed herself. The confidence that I've grown to have as a mom exists largely because I had her as a role model. I tell friends, "Everyone needs a 'Gisele' in her life." Her influence has helped me learn to shrug off the tantrums and the wipeouts, the spills and the foul moods. It's helped me aspire to be the kind of mom who can lower things to a simmer rather than raise them to a boil. I'm not there yet—not all the time, anyway. But because of her, I'm closer than I'd otherwise be.

In the end, we were told that Taylor would be okay. Turns out that chowing down on dozens of vitamins at once isn't exactly recommended—but it's something her body could handle. I felt a wave of relief, and a bit of regret at how I'd responded.

I look at Taylor, and I see a lot of myself. So many of the same qualities. Maybe that's the source of some of our run-ins. It's stubborn going up against stubborn. Hothead versus hothead. Things can get heated pretty quickly when both sides are adding fuel to the fire.

I don't think I can ever fully match my own mother's unflinching sense of calm. We're never going to be exactly the same. But maybe I can try a little harder and get a little closer to the mom who keeps her cool and always says, "It'll all work out. It'll be fine."

TWENTY-EIGHT

There's No Right Way to Be a Mom— There's Only Your Way

Nat and I didn't do very well in school. We didn't like reading the old novels and plays that we were ordered to read. But when we got pregnant, both of us were freaked out enough that we went on-line and bought the books that basically everybody buys. You know the ones. As I got closer to having my first child, I remember having this feeling like I was about to walk in to take a final exam—except I'd never been to class! I had no clue how to be a mother. I was look-ing for help, and I was willing to listen to anyone.

Nat and I later talked about how we both found the advice in these books to be so . . . I don't know what the right word is . . . rigid? Does that make sense? What I mean is that the authors all wrote as if they were the Gods of Parenting—the only ones with all the answers. There was never any wiggle room with these people! It was always "You've got to do it this way or else." You've got to feed them this way or else. You've got to discipline them this way or else. I found that surprising and a total turnoff. I mean, who died and made this dude the all-knowing expert? Sure, he has nine university degrees, but who is he to tell me how to raise *my* baby?

An even bigger problem was that these "experts" hardly ever agreed on anything. I'll give you an example. One of the books said that if your baby cries in the night, you need to go pick her up right away. Basically, if you don't pick up and soothe your baby right away, you are the worst mom ever and pretty much guilty of child abuse. Then, literally the next day, I was flipping through a book by another genius, who said you absolutely, 100 percent should *not* pick up your baby if she cries in the night. If you pick up your baby, she'll never learn to fall asleep and she'll still be waking up at three o'clock in the morning when she's eight years old.

So what exactly is a mom supposed to do with that information? I've got two know-it-alls and two bestselling books—and two completely different sets of instructions. No matter what I do, I'm doing the right thing *and* the wrong thing. I'm the best mom ever *and* the worst mom ever.

The contradictions went on and on. Let your kids be bored because it will allow them to take initiative and develop their creativity and imagination. But don't let them get too bored because then they'll get into drugs! Make sure you go back to work because you need to set a good example as an independent woman who can take care of herself. But also stay home because your kids need their mom.

This caused me a shitload of stress (pardon my language, but it's warranted here because I was *really* stressed out). I went looking for answers and basically left with a thousand questions and a million fears. Thanks for nothing, books!

I've already told you what a mess I was after our first daughter was born. I was constantly looking online for tips and guidance because I had no confidence that anything I was doing was right. Looking back, I'm sure Olivia could sense my uncertainty and my anxiety. It was only after I reconnected with Nat and we started to spend time together that things began to change. I began to understand that there is no perfect way to be a mother. There is no magical formula or flowchart that you have to follow. There is no single style or technique. Two women can both be nailing it at being moms—and they can be doing it in completely different ways. The key is finding the style that works for you and your kids.

Nat and I are best friends. We see each other every day. We have literally never had a fight. And yet our parenting styles are pretty different. In some ways, they are completely opposite.

What do I mean? Well, Nat is a yeller. She will use volume and theatrics to make her point and get her kids' attention. It works for her. Nat's kids are used to it, and they respond to it. They know when Mom is mad—and they know what that means. I hardly ever raise my voice. But that doesn't mean my kids don't know when I'm putting my foot down. They've learned from experience that just a subtle change in how I say something can mean all the difference.

Here's another example: Nat is big into praise. She builds her kids up that way. If they do okay at something, she acts as though they've just dominated the Olympics. She sees it as an effective way to encourage them and make sure they keep working hard, be it at school or at sports.

I'm more of a realist. I have zero problem being brutally honest with my kids about their lives and their accomplishments. There are a lot of parents out there who try to protect their kids from reality, which seems very weird to me. These days, it seems like every kid gets a ribbon or a medal at every event. We know a dad who was cleaning out his son's closet and found thirty-three medals or trophies from the boy's eight years in hockey. And, by the way, please take notice of the fact that all these "awards" were stuffed away out of sight. The kids are aware of which medals mean something and which ones were handed out to everyone who showed up.

And guess what? Not everybody is great at everything. Someone has to finish last. That may not be fun, but it's real life. I remember Olivia coming home one day with a participation ribbon. She presented it to me like she'd won a world championship. "I did really well, Mommy. I was the best." And I was totally frank with her. "No, babe. You didn't win. You lost. The other girl won. But if you want to get better, we can help you practice."

Nat sometimes literally laughs out loud when she hears me talking like this. Her way works for her. My way works for me. Don't get me wrong: I *do* celebrate my children in a whole bunch of ways. I am supportive, and I am their biggest fan when they are putting themselves out there. But I also want them to know that if I go wild for something they've done, they must have actually done something truly special.

Potty training is another good example. In some ways, Nat and I are in agreement. We have both come to realize—and remember, seven kids between us, so you can probably trust us on this!—that it's totally pointless to try to force a kid to use the potty before he or she wants to do it. It's much better to wait until they're ready—to hold off until they literally come up to you and say, "I want to go pee and poo on the toilet." If you start earlier than that, you're not going to get anywhere. Not in our experience, at least. They have to decide for themselves. With my son, I basically waited until he climbed up on the toilet on his own. I just found him sitting there with a look of determination on his face. He was ready.

So when my two-year-old daughter would come up to me and say, "I have to pee," I wouldn't rush her off to the bathroom. I wouldn't get all excited and switch into potty-training mode. I'd just say, "You have a diaper on. Go pee." I did that probably a hundred times—until one morning, she finally decided the time was right for her. "No, not in my diaper," she said. "In the toilet." She was ready.

I know what you're thinking. What if they're six years old and they're still fine taking care of their business in a diaper? Don't sweat it—they won't be. They just won't. If their own impulses don't lead them to the toilet, they'll be driven there by peer pressure. I'm talking about the good kind of peer pressure, where kids are inspired to grow up and make changes because they don't want to be the only ones who still take a dump in their pants.

So Nat and I agree on that much. We agree on waiting. But here's where we're different. Once a kid decides he's ready and starts trying, Nat moves into bribery mode. Starting right from our first couple of kids, she had this massive stash of gummy bears—and she'd hand them out every time her Taylor or my Olivia would use the toilet. It was ridiculous. It got to the point that Olivia would literally save it up if she knew we were going to Nat's house later on. I mean, why poo for free when you can get paid in gummy bears? She certainly wasn't getting any rewards at home. My philosophy was basically "You put it in the toilet? Whatever. Everybody does it. Are you expecting a medal or something?"

But here's the thing: I don't think my way is necessarily the *right* way. It just happens to be the right way for me and my kids. Nat's methods work for her. Sure, she now has to carry around a purse that's crammed with about eight pounds of candy—but she likes her method, and her kids respond to it. Bribery has become one of the tools she uses as a mom. If her kids don't want to leave the park to go home, she may choose to offer them a reward if they come along quietly. It helps to avoid conflict. Whereas I am much more of a mind to say, "If you don't leave the park with me right now, we're not coming back tomorrow." So, yeah, you can see why all my kids prefer Nat.

I guess what I'm trying to say is: There is no right way to be a mother. There is only your way. The bad news: You have to figure that out on your own. The good news: You *will* figure that out on your own.

TWENTY-NINE

Every Stage of a Child's Life Is Different and Also a Pain in the Butt

Just the other morning, everything seemed to be going so well. Cat and I spent several hours doing everything for our children—feeding them, playing with them (ugh), entertaining them. We said no one time—once!—and here's how Cat's daughter replied: "It's not fair. It's like you're the queen and you just sit on your throne with your tiara ordering us all around. You know what I'm going to do? I'm going to go pee on your bed."

Another day of living the dream!

There's a famous quote that I remember hearing in a movie or TV show. I looked it up online just to make sure I got it right: "Insanity is doing the same thing over and over again, but expecting different results." Some people think Einstein said it, but I have my doubts. It sounds more like something that would be said by a mom with little kids.

Think about it: Who does more things—lunchtime, bath time, bedtime—over and over again than a mom? Who wakes up every morning thinking (wrongly) that maybe, just maybe, things will be different today? Who the heck knows more about a world of absolute insanity?

Let's take a moment to look quickly at the first six stages of child-hood, as seen through the (tired, puffy) eyes of a mom:

Stage 1: The Baby Stage

Consists of: Sleepless nights. Constant crying. Endless feedings. Screaming (by both child and mother). Whining. Biting anything or anyone in sight. This nightmare eventually leads into the Awful Ones, during which the now-mobile child walks and runs off ledges, stairs, and all other structures that may cause harm, because what's life if you're not living it on the edge?

Stage 2: The Terrible Twos

Consists of: Talking without any logic and making absolutely no sense. Throwing, hitting, and expressing himself through any other form of violent, aggressive behavior. You spend most of the Terrible Twos wondering if your child is legitimately psychotic.

Stage 3: The Threenager

Consists of: Strong opinions from a stubborn, tiny terrorist, among other things . . .

Stage 4: The Friggin' Fours

Consists of: Hating you for everything that happens in her life, whether it's in your control or not. Being the biggest jerk because she just can't handle when things aren't exactly how she wants them.

Stage 5: The Fibbin' Fives

Consists of: Lying. Lying all the time. Exaggerating, bullshitting, completely making stuff up. It's all about finding out where the boundaries are—and trying to push beyond.

Stage 6: The Sassy Sixes

Consists of: Talking (and laughing hysterically) about private parts, the birds and the bees, and any other inappropriate thing that comes to mind. Asking awkward questions at awkward moments.

There are two things that remain consistent through all these stages:

1. Each stage is bonkers (just in a slightly different way).

2. Moms get the brunt of it.

Most kids are totally obsessed with, and focused on, their mothers. Here's a question for all the kids out there: What about Daddy? Why don't you go and bug him for a while?

Here is a true story: One of our kids was on the couch, snuggled in with his father with the TV on. I was upstairs taking a poop. (I know, I know—I'm making my life sound *soooo* glamorous.) The kid hopped down from the couch, marched upstairs, barged in on me in the bathroom, walked right up to me on the toilet, and asked: "Can you find me a different show?" Oh, I'm sorry—has something happened to your father? Does he no longer understand the English language? Has he lost the ability to push a few buttons on the remote? Also, get out of here because *I am pooping*.

Can you believe that? The kid was sitting *right next* to his father—and still he came to the conclusion that I was the only person on the planet who could solve his problem. That drove me insane! And it's not the only thing. Here is an evolving list of kid actions known to make this mom lose her shit:

Kid who needs to go to the bathroom . . . five minutes after I asked if she needed to go. We finally get to the restaurant. We settle in for a meal. And like clockwork, one of them announces, "I have to poo." Oh, and guess who has been requested as the chaperone for this exciting journey? Mommy, of course. Never Daddy. By the time we're back at the table, my food is cold and my white wine is lukewarm.

Kid who won't say please or thank you. It's weird. He can find the right word easily enough when he *wants* something: "Please, please, please, oh please, Mommy, please!" But when it comes time to master some simple courtesy, he just can't spit it out. He's going to be thirty-five years old and I'll still be trailing behind him, going "What's the magic word?"

Kid who asks for a snack about ninety seconds after finishing lunch. You think I'm exaggerating. Find any random mom and ask her if I'm exaggerating. I'm not exaggerating. The kid who takes two bites of her lunch and proclaims herself "full" is the same kid who in the next breath whines, "I'm hunnnnngry."

Kid who sits in a room crammed with at least two hundred toys and has the nerve to say, "I'm bored." Without a doubt, I drove my own mom crazy with this. But that was in the days before kid tech, interactive Pokémon, and robot buddies. It's good for kids to be bored, I know. I tell them so. But that doesn't mean I'm patient and understanding when they bellyache about it.

Kid who has thirty-five different T-shirts and comes out of his room saying, "I've got nothing to wear." The first law of motherhood is that a child's favorite shirt—the only shirt she ever wants to wear—will always be at the bottom of the laundry pile, covered in at least six different kinds of stains, four of which cannot be identified. Trying to reason with her that her other thirty-four shirts are just as good is a lost cause. It never works. Ever. She's just got to have the one with the orange dinosaur that happens to be covered in ketchup, mayonnaise, and . . . is that a booger?

Kid who fails to hang up a wet towel. The boy can instantly master the most complex and detailed video game. But it would appear that he is utterly baffled by the concept of a hook. (It's possible he picked this up from my husband, who is the worst offender.)

Kid who either refuses or can't remember to flush a toilet: "Did you flush the toilet? Did you wash your hands? Did you put down the seat? Did you brush your teeth? Did you turn out the light?" Over and over again. Are you starting to get my point about insanity?

Kid who says, "Just five more minutes!" Four more words that have the ability to send me over the top. Admittedly, my kids learned them from me. How dare you use my words against me? But here's the thing: Kids have no idea how long five minutes is. You tell them their five minutes is up and they think you're lying.

Kid who starts a fight in the backseat of the car. Can we all agree that the drive between school and home is never short enough? After an entire day of school, when they are not together, my kids will jump into the car and, twenty seconds into the ride, start to rip each other's heads off. Why are they fighting? About what? It doesn't matter. They might not even know themselves. History just repeats.

The other day, a friend who now has teenagers was telling me that her two kids used to be the same kinds of holy terrors. But now they sit quietly in the back of the car, each of them wearing earbuds, both of them in their own little worlds. She says she kind of misses the mayhem. For a moment, I thought: "Yeah, I get that." It made me kind of wistful to think that, one day, my little, wild ones may be silent and sullen. I actually got a tear in my eye. Then it occurred to me. One day, I'll also get dragged to a restaurant bathroom with my kids for the very last time. And I smiled.

THIRTY

So, Yeah, I Was Raised in a Shack with an Outhouse for Real

I have no memory of my parents ever being together as a couple.

They split up when I was just two years old. After the divorce, family life involved a lot of back-and-forth. My two older brothers and I would spend half our time at our dad's nice house in a swanky neighborhood in the heart of Toronto. Sometimes we'd go skiing for the weekend. Then we'd pack up and head to our mother's place. Mom did not live in a swanky neighborhood. She didn't live in a neighborhood at all. In fact, for a couple years, she lived an hour north of Toronto in something that barely qualified as a house.

Let me paint you a picture, okay? We're in the woods. Deep in the woods. Like Bear Grylls *deep* in the woods. And there's this cute little cabin. Or maybe you might take one look and call it a shack. Either way, we called it home.

I didn't have my own bedroom. Neither did my brothers. That's because there *were* no bedrooms. The cabin was made up of just one big room. I was four years old at the time—and my mom, my brothers, and I would eat in that room, live in that room, play in that room, and sleep in that room. Mom got the couch. The three of us kids crashed together on a mattress on the floor. Our only heat came from a woodstove in the middle of the room (seriously). Our only bathroom was . . . well, put on your shoes and bundle up if it's cold outside. The "toilet" for our one-room, deep-woods cabin was a nearby outhouse.

Jealous much?

Living in the woods brought its own unique challenges. I remember the first time my grandma came to visit. We decided to make chocolate chip cookies. We set out the ingredients, followed her recipe, and then opened our little oven to grab a baking sheet—

at which point a mouse bolted out. (Yes, we still baked the cookies, and they were *awesome*.)

My brothers would climb trees and go fishing, disappearing for hours at a time. They used to joke that they were raised by wolves. I was younger and had to stay closer to home. My brothers and I would scrounge for loose change—in the car seats, in the couch, in the woods, on the streets. Every nickel and dime brought us closer to the fifty cents we each needed to go swimming back in civilization at the local community pool.

Our one and only "luxury" was a small black-and-white TV with rabbit ears. We were allowed to watch it only on Sunday nights, when *The Wonderful World of Disney* came on. That was the full extent of our "screen time." Most Sundays, Mom would keep it on to watch *Murder, She Wrote*, which my brothers and I thought was a dumb show. How did this crazy woman always wind up being in the vicinity of a homicide? Seemed pretty suspicious to us.

I want to be superclear about something: My mother chose this way of living. When she and my dad split up, she refused to accept any kind of financial support. She simply wouldn't take his money. Mom said it was a question of principle. You can decide for yourself if you think that's admirable or nuts—but I've always been blown away by my mom's sense of independence and her confidence in her own ability to get the job done as a parent. One day, when I was all grown up and the cabin was a distant memory, she told me: "I didn't have a lot of money when you were young—and the money that I had, I wanted to spend it to give my kids an interesting life . . . a childhood they'd never forget." Mission accomplished, Mom!

Here's the unusual thing: It didn't seem weird at the time. We were kids—we just accepted it. This was the only routine we knew, so it felt normal to us. We didn't feel deprived. We didn't feel short-changed. If anything, we felt sorry for the other kids at school, who didn't have a backyard that went on forever.

Later on, my mom moved to another cabin, a little closer to civi-lization. At the time, she was working a full-time job in the city as a secretary at a bank. But it still wasn't easy to make ends meet—so she also got a job delivering newspapers. It was one of those rural routes you'd have to do in your car. Problem: She had to deliver the papers before sunrise at a time when she was raising three young children. Solution: She took us with her.

Every morning, we'd get up at 5:00, stuff the flyers into the newspapers (I always hated that part—my hands would get so black from the ink!), and then slide each paper into a blue bag. We'd all pile into Mom's little car, and off we'd go. My brothers loved the chal-lenge of trying to get the paper to land on the porch. I loved being with my family, the people I cared for most in the world. I know it seems like a kind of crazy way to live, but I accepted it. Actually, I did more than accept it. It was my life—our life—and I loved it. It seemed perfect to me.

So, yes, my upbringing was pretty far from typical. But the way I see it, my experience was more universal than you might think. Kids are resilient. They are way more flexible than we give them credit for. They can adapt to just about anything. For years, my brothers and I shuttled between one of the fanciest neighborhoods in Toronto and a clapboard hut where our closest neighbor turned out to be a bank robber on the lam. (The cops swooped in and busted him one day—much more excitement than we'd usually get in the woods!)

Not long ago, I met a single mom who was feeling low. You

could see it in her eyes and hear it in her voice. She seemed defeated. She told me, "I'm trying to be a mother *and* a father—and I feel like a failure at both." That can be such a crippling feeling. We all know it. Whether you're a single mother or you have a partner, every small mistake you make as a parent can eat at you. Every bad moment when you're not your best self can haunt you. Everyone has low points. Everyone gets frustrated. Everyone wonders, "Am I being a good mom?"

But kids don't care about our issues or our worries. They don't care about the pressures we put on ourselves. Most of them don't really care about what kinds of beds they're sleeping in or how many of them are in a room or any of the luxuries that we are encouraged to think are so important. They care about *us*. They love *us*. We're their moms!

Your situation may seem less than perfect to you. Or you may be living in a way that's different from most people. But to your kids, it's normal. It's their life. It's all they know. I never thought worse of my mother because of where we lived or how we spent our time. I never thought worse of my mother because she didn't buy me the latest cool toy or take me to Florida on spring break. Take it from someone who spent two winters pooping in an outhouse: What kids remember most is the love. Our mother loved us fully and passionately. We knew we were her top priority. We knew we were the best part of her life.

The details of daily life will fade. Whole years will be reduced to just a handful of memories. But kids will never forget how much, and how hard, you loved them. Sometimes your situation isn't ideal. Sometimes you can't afford a lot. Sometimes you open the oven and out pops a mouse. It doesn't matter. So long as your kids are loved, they have everything they need.

THIRTY-ONE

Don't You Dare Deny the World Your Mom Bod!

Nat

It was a brutally cold winter day, but I had a huge smile on my face. Nothing could wipe it off—not a house full of sniffling kids, not even a boot full of snow from when I stepped into a drift while trying to get into the car. I was so happy that I was singing out loud, even in the grocery store. In only forty-eight hours, Cat and I (and our husbands) would be heading to Mexico for a few days of sun, alcohol, warmth, alcohol, adult conversation (!), and—best of all—the tantalizing prospect of not being woken up before dawn by a crying child. It sounded like paradise. Also, there would apparently be alcohol.

My suitcase was already packed. It had been packed for days. I'd precooked a huge batch of food for the kids to be fed while we were away. There was only one item left on my pre-vacation to-do list. I looked at it—and my smile instantly started to fade. The last item on the list? Four of the most terrifying words known to the female mind: *Shop for a swimsuit.*

Here is a complete list of the things I, as the mother of four children, would rather do than try on swimsuits:

1. Literally everything else you can possibly even imagine.

The years pass. The kids begin to grow up. But I (and, I think, many moms) feel self-conscious about my body, just like in the weeks after giving birth. Finding the styles and colors that I like—that's the easy part. The fun part. Then comes the *next* part. Moms like me think of the changing room at a bathing suit store the way kids think of a haunted house. You dread it. You hesitate. You try to talk your way out of it. You know you're going to be shocked or horrified by something that you see. And you rush like hell to get out of there.

By the way: Who designs these places anyway? Could the light be any less flattering? It's bad enough I've got to see my naked body in three different mirrors—all of which are about two feet away from me. Do I also really have to strip off my clothes under the kinds of fluorescent bulbs that make me look every bit as healthy and radiant as a corpse?

I left the store with two expensive swimsuits—not because I buy big-name designers but because I want the suits that use the very latest technology to squish everything into a pleasing shape. Good work, scientists! But that wasn't enough for me. To my eyes, the swimsuits still left too much of me exposed. So I also sprang for a couple of matching cover-ups that I could wrap around my waist. They would keep my thighs cloaked from prying eyes.

Days later, we were at the hotel pool. We'd made it! The sun was shining. The drinks kept coming. And there I was, lying on a lounge chair with my legs bundled up and out of sight. I looked like a kid getting ready to shuffle to school in snow pants. After a couple hours—thanks to the combination of several white wines and some "friendly" encouragement from Cat ("Show us your sexy lady legs!" she kept yelling)—I finally decided to peel off the cover-ups. "Fuck it," I said, probably a little too loudly. And guess what? The world didn't end. No one seemed to notice. Everyone was probably too busy worrying about what other people thought about how *they* looked. I tucked away the cover-ups—and they stayed tucked away for the rest of our vacation. I had come to a realization: *Wear the friggin' swimsuit.*

It would be inspiring and heartwarming for me to say that accepting a postpregnancy body is easy. The only problem? It's not—not for me, anyway. One day, you realize your baby is almost a year old, but your body still looks five months' pregnant. Not a great feeling.

After each pregnancy it's like starting from scratch—which is hard, because you know how hard it's going to be. It's a struggle between learning about your new body and reminiscing about your old one. What you obsess on in the mirror is a fun-house version of the person you used to be. Sometimes people will say to me, "Oh, wow, you look so great . . . for having had four kids." I don't really know what they're trying to say. Am I hot? Am I not? And, anyway, why are you even talking about how I look? I just met you!

After one of our kids, I was my heaviest ever—I mean, even heavier than I was at nine months' pregnant. I felt stuck and uninspired and a bit like a stranger in my own body. I felt like I might never get "myself" back. It wasn't even about the weight as much as it was about reclaiming my own life after bringing another one into the world.

But as goofy as it may sound, that moment in Mexico was a game changer for me. It finally just occurred to me: Ten years ago—before babies—I beat myself up about my body, but I'd give a lot to have that body now. Ten years from now, I'll be lucky to have the body I have today. It all needs to stop.

There was a time in my life that I would have simply refused to get into a swimsuit if I looked anything less than perfect. Or anything less than *my* definition of perfect, anyway. There was a time when I was so insecure that I would allow people to take only "above the neck" photos of me. From the conversations I've had with other women, this is all pretty normal.

In the years since I've reconnected with Cat and we've become BFFs, the two of us have started countless diets. One time we gave up sugar. That was hard. Another time we ate only meals from jars.

That was . . . weird. We've jumped from one get-thin gimmick or kick-ass boot camp to another, documenting "our journey" to better, healthier versions of ourselves. We've taken *sooo* many of those "before" photos—you know, like the ones from the weight-loss ads—but I still haven't gotten the "after" photo I've always imagined.

I'm not going to get it anytime soon, either. And I'm okay with that.

True story: There was a time when my kids thought I didn't know how to swim. They mentioned it to me one day in the car. They said I should come to swimming lessons with them so I could learn. And it made sense that they would think that way. They were always in the pool. I was always watching from the pool deck. They were splashing around in the waves. I was watching from the shore.

Here I was, a mom who would always tell her children: "Don't *not* try something because you're nervous about how you'll look or what other people will think." And I was sitting on the sidelines because I was anxious that some random stranger might have an opinion about my butt. It was time for me to follow the advice I'd been giving to my kids. It was time for me to realize that my insecurities were getting in the way of making memories of fun times shared with my kids. It was time for me to realize that wearing a bathing suit was a great way to show my kids that different bodies are all beautiful.

One of the underrated benefits of motherhood is how it helps you get out of your own head—and stop obsessing over stuff that, at the end of the day, doesn't really matter all that much. It's not some sort of epiphany or anything. It's not magic. It's just the reality of your days. When you're a mom, you just don't have the time or the mental bandwidth to deal with quite as much nonsense. Life has kicked you in the ass and loudly announced: "Girl, it's not just about you any-more." Forget about being the center of the universe. You're no longer even the center of your own life.

That can be kind of freeing. For me, it's a relief not to think con-stantly about my physical appearance—how I look and how others think I look. Now, it's out to the car in sweatpants. It's out to baseball with no makeup on. It's out to the lake with a smile and a one-piece swimsuit.

I've still got those cover-ups from Mexico, by the way. But I hardly ever wear them. I've decided to accept the fact that I am who I am. Maybe one day I'll once again be the hot blonde with the bangin' body. I hope so. At this point in my life, I'm a mother with four kids and a Mom bod.

But I'm off the pool deck and into the pool. I'm off the shore and into the waves.

THIRTY-TWO

You Will Want Things for Your Children— This Is What We Want for Ours

A friend tells us a story. She is driving her two boys to school, as she does each morning. They are seven and five. There is traffic, as there always is. The mother is stressed that she will be late, as she often is. A car in front stops on a dime at a yellow light, forcing the mom to slam on the brakes. She honks the horn. She opens her mouth to fire off some curse words, as she sometimes does. Okay . . . as she *usually* does. But before she can say anything, she hears from the backseat, in the sweet voice of a seven-year-old boy: "For fuck's sake, buddy!" The boy doesn't know he's just dropped the f-bomb. He just knows from experience that these are the right words to say at this moment.

Kids learn by seeing and by listening and by doing. They mimic our behaviors, our gestures, and our words. If we swear, they will learn to swear. If we freak out when a plate is dropped, they will learn to freak out. At school, they learn facts. At home, they learn how to be the people they will one day become.

If we as moms are not living our lives with confidence and determination, there's no way our kids will have the guts to do so. These little people learn by watching. It's our responsibility not only to offer words of wisdom but also to live by what we believe. In other words, we can't just tell them how to be. We have to show them how to be.

When Nat and I first started to try to build a career together, there were people who thought we were crazy. (Heck, there are still people who think we're crazy!) We heard the word "no" a lot. Some didn't want to work with us. Others didn't even think we were worthy of a return phone call or email. But the two of us love going for more, and never settling for less. We kept at it. We worked hard. We fought for what we wanted in life. And we hope our sons and daughters will do the same.

We can't imagine not putting ourselves out there again and again. In making ourselves vulnerable, we have grown fierce in the fight against fears: the fear of judgment, the fear of change, the fear of failure, even the fear of success. We were scared of these things before we had kids. Once we became moms, we remained anxious. It wasn't until we started our own business that we began to win the battle. We realized that we can't grow, learn, create, succeed, or build fulfilling lives if we are afraid.

We have one rule we live by when it comes to fear: When we walk into a room, or meet someone new, we drop any preconceived judgments, notions, or ideas that we may have based on our own insecurities. We work really hard to always be positive, because we know too well that it's way too easy to judge. Against the doubters and the haters, we move forward. With luck, our children are absorbing these lessons in strength.

To be successful, you have to believe in yourself ten times more than your biggest doubter. You have to pick yourself up when the only thing you feel like doing is dropping out. You have to be ten times more confident than your biggest critic. That is true no matter what you hope to achieve in life—whether your goal is being the best stay-at-home mom for your children or becoming the boss at the company where you work.

If we had to choose a single quality to instill in our kids, it would be confidence.

"Do you. Just you," we tell them. "You are more than enough." We want them to be unafraid to be themselves and to seek out what *they* want from this life—not what others want for them.

We want them to be happy in their own skins, even if they're the odd ones out. We want them to know it's okay to zig when others are zagging. We want them to stand up for what they believe in. We want them to be kind.

We will also expect our children—if they follow our example—to be fearless in making their own decisions. We want them to trust their guts. We want them to give it all but know they can always change their minds. You can always begin again. "Just start," we always tell ourselves in such moments. "Stop talking and start doing."

We want our kids to embrace small moments. If they've learned nothing else in their unusual upbringing, they know how to rejoice. They know how to celebrate themselves and their families. And we hope they will never forget that very little in life can't be made better by a turn-it-up loud, spur-of-the-moment dance party.

Oh, and one last thing: We want them to be ready for when they fail.

God knows, we've made epic mistakes. Holy hell! We have days we're not proud of and about ten thousand moments we'd like back. Nat and I have never been afraid to fall down and get dirty. We hope our kids have been watching—because we always get back up and dust ourselves off. Every dang time.

Putting these words on this page is a useful reminder of what we want for our children. But it's our responsibility to do more than that. We have to show them how *we* live. We have to show them how we stay true to what we believe in. We have to show them the way so one day they can take the lead. And we have to try not to laugh out loud if one of them drops an f-bomb from the backseat.

CAT

THIRTY-THREE

Let Me Tell You About the Magical Day When I Got Four Whole Minutes to Myself

I'll be honest with you, okay? I wasn't ready for it. Not by a long shot. I'd dreamt about it. I'd imagined how I'd feel when it happened. But when the moment finally came, it took me *completely* by surprise.

It began as a typical summer morning. We were, as we say in Canada, "up north"—the part of the country known for its cottages, cabins, and resorts. It was 10:00 a.m. and already a scorcher of a day, so I made the easy decision and announced to the children: "Let's head to the pool!" Everyone cheered. Hooray—Mom's a genius and a hero!

The kids got into their swimsuits. And I . . . well, I did everything else, of course. I got the towels, found the sunscreen, tracked down the hats, packed the snacks, loaded the drinks, and reminded everyone about a hundred times to use the bathroom before we set off. (By my calculations, moms spend about 5 percent of their lives telling their kids to pee—and another 5 percent asking them why they didn't pee when they had the chance.) I slung one tote bag over my left shoulder and another over my right. I gripped the cooler with both hands. I felt just like a Sherpa—except instead of climbing Everest, we were walking in a straight line for about two hundred feet. Still, any outing with three young kids qualifies as an expedition.

Olivia jumped right into the deep end. She barely took the time to kick off her flip-flops. Max smooshed about a gallon of sunscreen onto his pasty white belly and entered with a cannonball. I finished sliding a set of Floaties onto Chloe's arms and turned to take off my floppy hat and T-shirt. Chloe was only two years old at the time—she would never even think about going into the pool on her own. She needed Mommy beside her, always within reach, even in the shallowest part of the shallow end. She liked the water, but that didn't stop her from having a death grip on my arm at all times. Chloe craved the security of Mom.

I turned back just in time to see Olivia emerge, grab her little sister by the hand, and slowly escort her into the pool. Chloe went willingly with a smile on her face. It took me a moment to process what I was witnessing. For the first time—the *first* time—my kids were swimming . . . and I wasn't in the pool. I stood there in disbelief. I didn't know what to do. I remember literally saying out loud to myself: "Is this for real right now?"

Eventually, I sat down in a chair. That's how I celebrated this latest milestone in the growth and development of my children. I sat down in a chair and enjoyed the rare feeling of doing absolutely nothing.

It was totally frickin' great.

Now, I don't want you to get the wrong idea. I did not order a cocktail, read a trashy novel, or doze off for an hour. Not a chance. When you're the mother of little kids, the pool is always going to be an area of High Alert. It doesn't matter if there are fifteen lifeguards—your eyes are darting around on a continuous loop: Olivia, Max, Chloe. Olivia, Max, Chloe. All accounted for. Pause to blink and . . . Olivia, Max, Chloe. Olivia, Max, Chloe.

But this was still pretty amazing. I was sitting on my own in the sun while my three children played together in a pool. Yes, I had to judge Max as he did about nine thousand jumps and dives. And yes, soon enough Olivia paddled off on her own into the deep end—and Chloe was once again calling for Mommy. But it was still an important moment. I took the time to recognize and appreciate it as it was happening.

And that's what I always try to do. It can be tempting as a parent to look forward with anticipation to each kid's next phase. How much more mature and independent they'll be. It can also be tempting to look back with nostalgia at how they used to be. How much smaller and cuter they were. Nat does this a lot. She's always asking other moms how much longer a certain irritating behavior is likely to last. She will reminisce about when her kids were younger. And that totally works for her. But the way I see it, if you spend your time focused on the future or the past, you risk missing out on what's happening in their lives right now. It might sound a little corny, but I try to stay in the moment.

That doesn't mean that I don't sometimes miss the simpler times—like when the questions coming from the backseat of the car were innocent and hilarious (Chloe: "Mommy, why is the sky just blue and not like a zebra?") As my kids get older, the questions are becoming much more . . . interesting.

Not too long ago, the five of us were crawling through the usual mess of Toronto traffic. We had some music playing. The backseat trio was quiet. I should have known that it couldn't last. Sure enough, out of nowhere, Olivia pipes up. "Daddy," she says, "when you first saw Mommy, did you feel the passion?"

Marc gripped the steering wheel tightly and gave me a side glance. His face somehow went red with embarrassment and white with panic at the exact same time. He mouthed three letters of the alphabet in my direction. I bet you can guess which ones.

W. T. F.

"Like, when you saw her," Olivia continued, unaware that she was on the verge of making her father's head explode, "what did you want to do with her? Did you want to do The Passion?" (I'm putting capital letters on The Passion because that's how Olivia said those two words—with great emphasis, as if she knew they were important.)

Under his breath, Marc said to me: "Why does our eight-year-old daughter know about 'The Passion'?" Out loud to the entire car, he said: "Hey, look at those trees over there. Those are nice, big trees." Olivia didn't care about Dad's stupid trees. "You know that thing that people do when they like each other—The Passion. Did you want to do that to Mommy?"

Marc swallowed hard, gave in to his fate, and began to answer the question. Well, he tried to answer it anyway. I think he started about nine different sentences and finished none of them. "When I met your mommy . . . When men and women like each other . . . Um, well, I guess I saw Mommy and I liked her and then . . ." Suddenly, Max was interested. "What do you mean 'The Passion'? How do you do The Passion?"

Yeah, no, it was clearly time for me to step in. In part, this was an act of mercy, because I'm pretty sure my husband was about to drive us straight into one of those nice, big trees so he wouldn't have to hear another word about The Passion. But it was also an act of self-preservation because it had suddenly dawned on me—Olivia had first heard talk of "passion" while lying in bed with me and watching an especially steamy episode of *The Bachelor*. (Oops.) I didn't want to overshare in front of the younger kids, so I just told Olivia, "Of course Daddy felt The Passion for Mommy. How could he not? Mommy is so awesome." Everyone laughed and we moved on. Except for Marc, who is probably still traumatized to this day.

This was only the beginning of the interesting questions. A couple weeks later, Olivia asked me about vaginas. Totally normal, obviously. We talked it out, as we always do. I'm always very up front with my kids (and Nat's kids . . . and your kids, if you need someone to give it to them straight). I'm happy to go as deep as they want to go into any topic. I don't get embarrassed. The only hitch is that little Chloe happened to be in the room at the same time—and to her ears, "vagina" was just about the most entertaining word she had ever heard in her entire life. So, she spent the next three days shouting it everywhere she went. That made for a rather awkward visit to the mall. But, hey, she's little and she's adorable—she can get away with shouting anything she wants. "Vagina! Vagina! Vagina!" It just makes people smile. Whereas when I do it, I get asked to leave Whole Foods. (Kidding.)

These questions from Olivia were a wake-up call for me. For years, my kids had relied on me solely for their physical needs. I was basically an assembly-line worker in the Factory of Mom: Cook this, wash that, comb this, wipe that. It was so dang repetitive and tiring. But the job didn't ask much of me in terms of brainpower.

Now, all of a sudden, I'm expected to know stuff! My kid is firing a zillion questions at me—and she's not settling for general answers. She wants deets. It's like, whoa, apparently I need to understand things about anatomy and animals and the universe and about a billion other topics. I need to figure out how I'm going to talk to my kids about sex and bodies and relationships. I need to figure out how I'm going to talk to them about their own feelings and desires and hang-ups—and what I'm going to say when they ask about religion and death. And I definitely need to come up with some good deflection techniques for when they ask me stuff that's way beyond me, like

"How does an iPhone actually work?" Max asked me that the other day. My answer? "How do *you* think it works?" Clever, right? Knock that ball right back over the net. It got me out of the jam this time, but it's only a matter of time until he'll be back for more. (Ladies, I have *no* clue how an iPhone works. I just assume either it's magic or there's a tiny little elf named Siri in there.)

For me, this is a whole new part of the parenting experience. Babies seem like miracles, but let's face it: They're pretty anonymous. It takes quite a few years until you can begin to say with confidence, "Yeah, I see what kind of person she's going to be. I see her personality taking shape and taking root. I see her character and her manner and her values and her preferences." With each day that passes, your kid is closer to the person that he or she is going to be. And the things we say, the decisions we make, the example we set as mothers—we help to shape these futures. It's a huge responsibility that I'm just beginning to get a handle on.

This is how it is with a child: Every couple of years or so, it's like getting to know an entirely new person. Nat's oldest is a great example. When Taylor was little, she was a total clinger. She lost it pretty much anytime her mother dropped out of sight. To be honest, it was kind of cute at first—what mom wouldn't love being *so* adored by her kid? But then it started getting uncomfortable. Nat would take Taylor to birthday parties—but she'd be forced to stick around, knowing that Taylor would freak out the moment Mommy made a break for the outside. Picture Nat sitting there in a little plastic chair, eating a tiny slice of cake with fifteen little girls. (This actually happened, by the way.) Picture the looks on the faces of the parents of the birthday boy when Nat informs them, "I know all the other parents are leaving, but I'm just going to stand here and make awkward chitchat with you guys for two hours because my daughter will literally scream for forty minutes if I so much as touch the exit door."

That's who Taylor was as a little girl. It was part of her journey. Yes, there were moments when Nat would say, "Is this it? Is she always going to be like this?" But two years later, Taylor was independent and confident. She had made good friends at school—and that changed everything. Today, she's as eager to ditch her mom as any pretween girl.

A couple years ago on Facebook, someone posted a quote that I've since seen all over the place. You've probably seen it, too. It goes something like "One day, without realizing it, you will pick up your child for the final time ever." It's the kind of Deep Thought that's supposed to give you all the feels. *Oh my God! My special little tiny baby is going to grow up! Oh, the horror of it all!*

Sorry, but that kind of stuff doesn't cut it with me. We *want* our kids to grow up, don't we? Isn't that the whole point? We want them to move on and move out—for their own good, and so that we can begin to reclaim our own lives, our own time, our own independence. I can't wait to lift my youngest kid up for the last time. It'll mean that Chloe and her siblings are closer to the people they were meant to become.

Our kids are changing all the time, with our help and guidance and influence. I don't ever push it. I wait patiently for each new display of independence—the beginning of each new stage in their lives. And when it happens, I don't get all weepy about how things used to be. After all, it's not like I'm losing them. I talk to my own mom almost every day, so believe me: I'm not going anywhere. My kids and I are tied together forever by blood and by family, by history and by love.

One day in the future, my kids will get old enough that they'll stop calling me "Mommy." But no matter what, I'll always be their mom.

THIRTY-FOUR

Having a Bad Day Doesn't Mean You're a Bad Mom

Nat

There was a moment. Your kid wasn't listening. You tried to reason with her. And then, because you're only human, you yelled at her. You really let her have it. She was shocked. Her eyes got wide and wet. She ran off, crying.

Maybe you went to bed that night feeling lousy about yourself. We've been there. *I've* been there. I've lain in bed thinking about what I should have done differently. I've felt waves of regret for not having shown more patience. It's healthy and it's useful to evaluate how we're doing as mothers—and to try to get even better. But here's what's important: The next moment is a new moment. The next day is a new opportunity.

Bring your kids back in. Let them know you love them. Start again.

As Cat and I look back now as mothers of seven children, that's just one of the things we wish we'd known from the start. We wish someone had prepared us for those complicated feelings. We wish someone had told us they were normal. So, we're telling you now. You're not a bad mom. You just had a bad day being a mom.

Discovering you are pregnant for the first time can send you hurtling at top speed into an all-consuming universe of questions, possibilities, hopes, fears, and unknowns. I don't care how many books you read. No one will ever have all the answers. Every single mother out there—including the seemingly perfect moms who appear to breeze through life—has highs and lows. Every mother has feelings of both joy and guilt.

Even the world's best moms have hard days. Days when your patience is just gone, and then your kids ask why you're mad at them—

and it breaks your heart because you're *not* mad at them. Of course you're not. You're just fried.

Being a mom often means not knowing. We know that now. We know about the hard times and anxious moments when you feel like you're about to break. We know that even in crowded, hectic days surrounded by little people, it is possible to feel alone.

We also know that the crazy parts of motherhood are normal. We know that finding two matching socks is overrated. And we know that it helps to share. As my final bit of sharing with you in this book, here are a few things that Cat and I wish we'd known at different stages of our Mom lives.

What We Wish We'd Known When . . . We Were Pregnant with Our First Babies

Sleep more. We wish we'd slept as though we might not get another chance for eighteen years.

Worry less. After seven kids, we know that the only thing you can *really* expect when you're expecting is that *your* experience and *your* labor will be impossible to predict. It will be okay. You will rock it.

Fully let go of life as we knew it. Things are never the same after kids. Rather than resisting the transition, we wish we'd spent that time anticipating the good, the bad, the hard, and the crazy.

Stop momsplaining things to dads. It took us waaaay too long to realize our husbands were never going to truly understand what it's like to be a mama or a mama-to-be. We wasted a lot of time trying to explain!

What We Wish We'd Known When . . .
We Were First-Time Moms of Newborns

Babies cry for no reason. Your baby will cry. She will wail. She may cry for so long that you begin to think, "Will she ever stop?" You will not always be able to figure out why she is crying. It's not about you.

Moms sometimes do the same. *You* will cry. You may not be able to figure out why. Seek out other new moms. Don't be afraid to start up a conversation. You may discover other moms are feeling the same way.

The sleepless nights will end. You will hope and pray and wish for the night your baby sleeps all the way through. We did, too. It will happen . . . eventually!

Everything will get easier. Even though it seems like you might not make it through the first year, you will survive. We did. And you will, too.

What We Wish We'd Known When . . .
We Were First-Time Moms of Toddlers

You may lose yourself. Maybe you thought this was everything you wanted in life. Maybe you thought it would complete you and make you feel whole. That may be true. But for a while, there's a chance you may forget about yourself and your own needs as you obsess over your toddlers. Take care of *you*, too.

You may judge other moms but shouldn't. As you grow more confident as a mom, you may think you're the only one who gets it. The only one who is making the right decisions. When you find yourself judged, you'll stop judging.

You will eventually master this. We promise that one day you will leave the house without having a mental breakdown along the lines of "Did I pack the right things? Did I remember everything? Is my shirt done up?"

You should trust yourself more. You love being a mom so much. You're good at it, too. Listen to yourself. Trust your instincts. Do what's right for your child, for you, and for your family. This is your journey and nobody else's.

What We Wish We'd Known When . . .
We Were First-Time Moms with a Toddler and a Newborn

The first year will still be hard. It won't matter that you've been through it before. Any way you cut it, it will be a challenge. But you're up to it!

The milestones will begin to blur. Even with seven kids between us, we still forget what's supposed to happen when. "Should she be sitting up by now? When can I stop breastfeeding? Damn, she just bit me! I guess it's time for her teeth to come in!"

Everything is a phase, even when it seems like it isn't. There will be good phases and there will be bad phases. Bad phases will be followed by amazing phases. And there will be *lonnnng* phases where you think your child will always insist on wearing his shoes on the wrong feet or making that weird noise with his tongue while he's watching TV. This tongue phase will actually seem charming when he becomes a teenager and goes through his heavy-metal-music phase.

You will be tired. We were better moms with newborns the second time around. We were better organized. We were in a place where, in theory, we could actually lie down and sleep when our babies dozed off. Except for one thing: the loud and demanding toddlers who refused to nap!

You can't kill it every day. Some days you'll nail it, and other days will be complete disasters.

What We Wish We'd Known When . . .
Our Firstborns Started School

They will be fine. It may look and sound like a mob scene when you drop them off that first day, but they'll be okay. Let them be okay. (And, yes, it's fine for you to bawl like a maniac *after* you drop them off and are back in your car.)

They will figure it out. They will learn to get ready, eat their snacks and meals, and make friends on their own. They don't need you there to help them, even though it kills you to accept this.

They will want you less but need you more. They don't always need you to fight their battles or solve all their problems. More than ever, they do need your love, your guidance, and your support.

No news is good news. Like us, you will want to grill the teacher at the end of every school day. Now we know that when the teacher waves from a distance and moves on, it means your kid is doing fine.

Kids can be mean. Your heart is going to shatter when your kids tell you about being left out, hanging out solo, or sitting by themselves at lunch. Don't make them the victims. Instead, celebrate that they are strong enough to play on their own. They will find others they want to be with and who want to be with them.

Some days it feels like we have it all figured out. The next day, we look up and there's a whole new wave of mothering challenges coming right at us. Some days are easy, others are so damn hard. You nail it, then you fail it. This is motherhood. This is life.

CAT

THIRTY-FIVE

You Are Mom Enough

At my mom's little cabin in the woods where I grew up, my brothers and I would disappear for hours at a time. When we'd go into the city to stay with our dad, it was the same story. We would roam the neighborhood without caring where we were going—or worrying about when we'd return. Back then, kids used to be parented in part by communities. You as a neighbor could yell at someone else's son or daughter, and it would be fine. Not today. Today it's, like, "Don't you dare talk to my kid that way!" We have become more protective and more isolated.

For the first time, motherhood has become a solo experience for many women. Until now, there has always been a tribe, a village, a neighborhood, a community. Everyone looked out for everyone else. Somewhere along the line, it began to be seen as "heroic" for a mother to do everything—have a full-time job, raise the kids, do it all on her own. It's certainly not viewed as "heroic" to ask for help. Which is ridiculous! If we're not allowed even to reach out, how can we not fail every day?

I'm lucky to have my mom and Nat. I'm lucky to have a great and supportive husband. But not everyone is that lucky. For some, the support isn't there. And our collective judgments have become harsher. Now, just by having a crying child in a public place, you may feel as though you have failed. The minute you lose your shit on your kids, you feel as though you have failed.

I know how it is to feel like a failure. But that feeling led me to a new way of thinking. Over time, I came to realize how important it is to ignore the judgments of others—and to trust your own instincts and your own confidence. You'll never be able to please everyone. You'll never be able to get it right all the time. So trust your gut and focus on the things you care about most. And help other moms trust *their* guts by being kind. We are more alone than ever in our society, and that's not a good thing. We need to build connections.

Have you ever watched any of those school graduation speeches on YouTube? You know how those things go, right? Some smart person puts on a black robe and a dumb hat and stands up on a stage and gives life advice to a bunch of young women and men who are just getting started in the world.

I've never been to one in person because they don't give you a fancy speech when you graduate from night school! But I was waaaay down a rabbit hole one day (it happens), and I stumbled on a speech by David Foster Wallace. I'd never heard of the guy. (I know there are a few of you out there going, "Cat! How? He's the best writer ever!" Which may be true, but I looked and his books are *gigantic*, so . . . no.)

Anyway, David is talking to a bunch of graduates. One of his points is that *you* control how you see your world. And you decide how you want to react. You can get pissed off when you're stuck in a long checkout line—or you can understand that everyone is in the same boat. You can judge the people around you harshly—or you can give them the benefit of the doubt.

He gives an example. He talks about the impulse to judge a mother he sees in a supermarket. "If you're aware enough to give yourself a choice," he says, "you can choose to look differently at this fat, dead-eyed, over-made lady who just screamed at her little child in the checkout line—maybe she's not usually like this; maybe she's been up three straight nights holding the hand of her husband who's dying of bone cancer, or maybe this very lady is the low-wage clerk at the Motor Vehicles Department who just yesterday helped your spouse resolve a nightmarish red-tape problem through some small act of bureaucratic kindness. Of course, none of this is likely, but it's also not impossible. It just depends on what you want to consider."

I think that's kind of beautiful. None of us knows another mom's truth. We don't know her fears or insecurities. We don't know how her morning went. We don't know how she was brought up. That goes for the high-performing, control-freak moms, too. We don't know what drives them, or the pressures they are under. We don't know what goes on in their heads—or how they feel about themselves and their lives. So maybe we should just give everyone (including ourselves) a break.

That really sums up what Nat and I try to do in our lives—and what we are trying to do with this book. As a mother, you may find it's tempting to see yourself as the center of the universe. It's easy to get frustrated and lash out. And it's very easy to judge others—to try to make yourself feel better by holding yourself up against someone you see as a lesser mom. Nat and I both did that. Nat used to live by a daycare, and we'd sometimes say to our children: "Look at those daycare kids—it's almost dinner and they're still there! I wonder where their mommies are." It made us feel better about the choices we had made. But it was also mean and petty.

Judging is a choice. As DFW (I Googled him and that's what the cool kids call him) put it, "You get to *decide* how you're going to try to see [life]. . . . You get to decide what to worship." It can be hard, because it may mean having to overcome our default settings. But we can choose to build up other moms, rather than tear them down. We can choose to support each other. We can choose to come together and make motherhood a sisterhood.

Imagine if we just chose to say, "Wow, you're doing a great job as a woman and a mom—no matter how you choose to mother your children."

Imagine if we just chose to trust that each mom is navigating this very judgmental world the best she can, doing the best she can, with the best interests of her kids at heart.

And imagine if we decided that, instead of beating ourselves up, we would celebrate ourselves. In fact, let's not just imagine it. Let's do it—right now!

Here's to the average, typical, ordinary, awesome, incredible, amazing mom!

Here's to the mom who said yes to a snack about two seconds after dinner because it was the path of least resistance . . .

. . . the mom who thought for sure it must be almost bath time but the stupid clock says it's only 3:30 (!) . . .

. . . the mom who stayed calm right through the extended dinnertime freak-out that started because the applesauce was (horrors!) slightly touching the meat . . .

. . . the mom who is keeping it together despite being short on patience, because the witching hour is really long some nights . . . like, really long . . .

. . . the mom who is hanging on by a thread with a frustrated grade schooler who needs help with homework but says you're not helping him the "right" way . . .

. . . the mom who was planning to get up in the morning as the best version of herself and be the world's best mom—but who was woken up in the night seven hundred times by one or multiple children and is now making it through the morning one coffee at a time while secretly waiting for nap time to come . . .

...the mom who laughs at the tiny disaster she's created, because it's all perfectly hers.

And here's to the mom who will single-handedly pick up the kids, make dinner from nothing, clean up, manage the fiery moods, give them individual attention, referee a hundred fights, sign a million forms, and organize where they all have to be (mostly on time), and then somehow wrangle them all to bed and then probably start on her own to-do list, even though she'd rather just fall down face-first on the bed.

There is nothing "average" about the average mom.

Through our own behavior, through our own actions, we are teaching our children how to deal with challenges of their own—and how to treat other people.

We love our kids. And that's what our kids will remember. That's the one constant they'll have from their time as children: how much, and how hard, you loved them.

Sometimes the floors are dirty and gross. Sometimes breakfast is from a drive-through. Sometimes their clothes are on backwards, or inside out, or not at all. It's fine. It's all fine. Let's all just be the moms we are.

Each and every day, we are responsible for meeting the needs of our kids. Each and every day, we make parenting decisions that we *hope* are right. Because let's be honest: No one *really* knows what's right and what's wrong. It's all a big, giant guess—and we can only hope that we make the right choice.

Nat and I are doing the best we can, the best we know how—which is really all we can do. That's what we tell each other when one of us is feeling down or defeated.

We are not perfect moms. We're not the moms who are super-organized. We're not the moms who always (or ever) remember the diaper bag. We're not the moms who set aside Sunday night to plan out every single meal for the entire week. Do we sometimes wish we had it all together? You bet. Do we sometimes work a little harder to be even better than we are? Yep.

But we have learned to embrace the chaos, not to fear it. We have learned to accept the mess, rather than stress about it. We have learned that sometimes we're going to zone out for five seconds and discover that the oldest is putting lipstick on her baby brother. Sorry, little guy. That one's on Mommy. My bad.

It's okay to be the mom you are. In fact, it's better than okay. It's perfect.

Want to know the ultimate Mom Truth? If you love your kids, you're mom enough.

 catandnat ...

All your kids want is you.

Not the fit mom. Not the Pinterest mom. Not the mom who runs the PTA or the mom with the fancy car or the mom who bakes muffins from scratch every Friday morning before dawn.

They don't want the mother you some-times think you should be. They don't want any other mother, no matter how nice she looks on Instagram.

All they want is you.

View all 235 comments

C + N

#MomTruth

ACKNOWLEDGMENTS

This is the part of the book where the authors usually thank everybody they've ever met in their entire lives.

Sorry, but we're moms. We don't have time for that. Let's keep it to the people who matter most.

Thanks to our awesome editor, Donna Loffredo, who helped us to tell our story.

Thanks to our own moms, Gisele and Sharon, for leading by example—and for showing each and every day how strong women and mothers can be.

Thanks to our children—Taylor, Olivia, Teddy, Tucker, Max, TJ, and Chloe—for the love, for the encouragement, and for leaving us alone in the bathroom every now and then (but still not always).

Thanks to Marc and Mark (our guys, our hubs) for understanding that we chose them—but that, as moms and as friends, we need each other.

Most of all, we want to thank all of you—the moms who follow us, who communicate with us, who watch us online, who come to our shows. The moms who share with us their joys and their anxieties, their laughter and their love. You made it possible for us to write this book. You keep us going. You inspire us every dang day.

ABOUT THE AUTHORS

CATHERINE BELKNAP and NATALIE TELFER have been friends since they were teens but grew closer after motherhood when they chose to confide in each other about the more taboo topics of parenting. It wasn't long afterward that they decided to bring the conversation online in hopes of helping other moms feel less isolated. Their rapidly-exploding community of like-minded moms tune in every day to watch them rewrite the paradigm of "the perfect mom." Cat and Nat share everything that moms think but are too afraid to talk about. Find them online at catandnat.ca or on all social media channels @catandnat.